The Book of Isaiah

OneBook.

DAILY-WEEKLY

The Book of Isaiah

Chapters 56–66

John N. Oswalt

Seedbed

Printed in the United States of America

Cover design by Strange Last Name
Page design by PerfecType, Nashville, Tennessee

Oswalt, John.
    The Book of Isaiah : chapters 56-66 / John N. Oswalt. – Frankin, Tennessee : Seedbed Publishing, ©2018.

        pages ; cm. + 1 videodisc – (OneBook. Daily-weekly)

        ISBN 9781628245004 (paperback)
        ISBN 9781628245042 (DVD)
        ISBN 9781628245011 (Mobi)
        ISBN 9781628245028 (ePub)
        ISBN 9781628245042 (uPDF)

        1. Bible. Isaiah, LVI-LXVI -- Textbooks. 2. Bible. Isaiah, LVI-LXVI -- Study and teaching. 3. Bible. Isaiah, LVI-LXVI -- Commentaries.   I. Title. II. Series.

BS1520 .O86 2018 v.3   224/.106   2018934623

SEEDBED PUBLISHING
Franklin, Tennessee
seedbed.com

CONTENTS

CONTENTS

CONTENTS

WELCOME TO ONEBOOK DAILY-WEEKLY

John Wesley, in a letter to one of his leaders, penned the following:

> O begin! Fix some part of every day for private exercises. You may acquire the taste which you have not: what is tedious at first, will afterwards be pleasant. Whether you like it or not, read and pray daily. It is for your life; there is no other way; else you will be a trifler all your days. . . . Do justice to your own soul; give it time and means to grow. Do not starve yourself any longer. Take up your cross and be a Christian altogether.

Rarely are our lives most shaped by our biggest ambitions and highest aspirations. Rather, our lives are most shaped, for better or for worse, by those small things we do every single day.

At Seedbed, our biggest ambition and highest aspiration is to resource the followers of Jesus to become lovers and doers of the Word of God every single day, to become people of One Book.

To that end, we have created the OneBook: Daily-Weekly. First, it's important to understand what this is not: warm, fuzzy, sentimental devotions. If you engage the Daily-Weekly for any length of time, you will learn the Word of God. You will grow profoundly in your love for God, and you will become a passionate lover of people.

How Does the Daily-Weekly Work?

Daily. As the name implies, every day invites a short but substantive engagement with the Bible. Five days a week you will read a passage of Scripture followed by a short segment of teaching and closing with questions for reflection and self-examination. On the sixth day, you will review and reflect on the previous five days.

Weekly. Each week, on the seventh day, find a way to gather with at least one other person doing the study. Pursue the weekly guidance for gathering. Share learning, insight, encouragement, and most important, how the Holy Spirit is working in your lives.

That's it. Depending on the length of the study, when the eight or twelve weeks are done, we will be ready with the next study. On an ongoing basis we will release new editions of the Daily-Weekly. Over time, those who pursue this course of learning will develop a rich library of Bible learning resources for the long haul.

OneBook: Daily-Weekly will develop eight- and twelve-week studies that cover the entire Old and New Testaments. Seedbed will publish new studies regularly so that an ongoing supply of group lessons will be available. All titles will remain accessible, which means they can be used in any order that fits your needs or the needs of your group.

If you are looking for a substantive study to learn Scripture through a steadfast method, look no further.

INTRODUCTION

Righteousness: The Character of Servanthood

The final section of the book of Isaiah, chapters 56–66, seems to be very strangely constructed. In many ways the climax of the section, and even the book, occurs in chapters 60–62, with the following chapters, 63–66, being almost anticlimactic. So we, the readers, wonder what is going on.

While I was working on the first of my commentaries on Isaiah, I came across a suggestion by a French writer that made a great deal of sense to me, and the longer I have worked with it, the more probable it seems to me. The suggestion was that the section is constructed chiastically. A chiasm is something like a literary triangle in which the elements in the two upright sides parallel each other, with both pointing to the main point at the center. It looks something like this:

$$D$$
$$C \qquad C$$
$$B \qquad\qquad B$$
$$A \qquad\qquad\qquad A$$

The two A parts are saying similar things; the B parts are saying something else, but both are making the same point, and the same is true for the C parts. Here in Isaiah 56–66 there are five parts, and the thought line goes like this: (A) righteous foreigners (56:1–8; 66:18–24); (B) unrighteous Israel (56:9–59:15a; 63:7–66:17); (C) Divine Warrior defeats sin (59:15b–21; 63:1–6); (D) The Light shines through righteous people (60:1–22; 61:4–62:12); (E) The Messiah (61:1–3). So the segment begins and ends (A) with the thought that has run through the book from the very beginning: Israel has a mission to the nations—to make it possible for them to see Yahweh's glory, to live in his presence, and to share his character. This is the foundation thought; this is why God called them and redeemed them: that the world might know him. But in fact, (B) Israel has been sinful; they have not displayed the character of God;

moreover, they seem unable to do so. What is to be done? (C) The Warrior will come from heaven and with his own righteousness defeat the power of sin in his people's lives. What will be the result? (D) Like a lantern whose lenses and globe have been stringently cleaned, the Light will shine out of them for all the world to see. Who is the Warrior who makes this possible? (E) None other than the Spirit-anointed Messiah of whom the book has been speaking throughout.

Now why make these points in this chiastic fashion? I think it is so that we will not forget what the issues are. Salvation is not about us; it is about the world. Nor dare we ever forget that in us, as the apostle said, "dwelleth no good thing" (Rom. 7:18 KJV). If the light of Christ is ever to shine out of us for the world to see, it will be his doing in our tender and contrite hearts, and nothing of ours. By reiterating these points in this manner, Isaiah underlines them in a memorable way.

Many scholars believe that these chapters are addressed to the people who returned from the Babylonian exile circa 538 BC. It certainly seems like what is taught here would fit that time. It is very possible that those returnees were saying, "Why are we back in the land? It had nothing to do with us; it was just the grace of God. We are the chosen people, so it doesn't matter how we live." On the contrary, said Isaiah, it does matter how God's servants live. He calls us into a relationship with himself, a relationship that is impossible if we do not share his character. Yet it is not possible for us to reproduce that character by ourselves. It must be done by God himself as we surrender ourselves to him. This is very much the same message that is found in Romans 6–8.

At the same time, there is very little in these chapters that is specific to Israel in the years after 538. The point being made is governed more by theology than by a particular historical setting. What the prophet was attempting to do was to synthesize the apparently disparate teachings of chapters 1–39 and 40–55. Chapters 1–39 insist that God's people must live righteous lives. If they did not, they would go into exile, as they did. But chapters 40–55 say almost nothing about righteous living. Instead, these chapters speak of *God's* righteousness in graciously delivering his people from the consequences of their sin. If the book had ended at chapter 55, we might very well conclude that in view of God's grace, righteous living is of little consequence. What chapters 56–66 are doing is putting the two messages together. God himself will graciously enable us to fulfill the call to righteous living. Yes, we must live righteous lives, but we are enabled to do so by his grace alone.

Because it is difficult to adhere to the chiastic structure in the format of these lessons, I will be combining some of the parallel sections as we move through, seeking to give you the key points that are being made on both sides of the chiasm.

WEEK ONE

Isaiah 56:1–57:2; 66:14–24

Righteous Foreigners;
Unrighteous Israel

INTRODUCTION

Christians everywhere agree that we are delivered from the consequences of our sins and brought into fellowship with God by his grace as a result of our faith in Christ (Eph. 2:8–9). But what then? Most will agree that we ought to live more Christlike lives as a result of that deliverance and fellowship. But differences arise when we ask whether such Christlike character is an expectation or not. Some, perhaps a majority today, will say that while it is indeed desirable, and is a necessary goal for which we should strive, it is not really achievable in this life. But the unfortunate practical effect of this position is that many Christians today do not expect to live godly lives and make very little effort in that direction.

Isaiah understood that this is what would happen to the Judeans who were miraculously delivered from exile in Babylon and allowed to return to Jerusalem and Judah. They would recognize that they had gone into exile as a result of their persistent rebellion against Yahweh and their continual breaking of their covenant with him. They had failed to live the kind of righteous lives that the covenant called for (chaps. 1–39). So why had they been delivered? Was it because they had gotten their act together, repented, and begun to live more righteously? There is no indication of that. What many of them did do, it seems, was to believe God's promises of deliverance and to refuse to merely be absorbed into Babylonian culture. (That is, they had faith.) So, once they were back in their own land, there was great danger that they would conclude, as have many modern Christians, that it really did not matter whether they lived conspicuously godly lives or not. It is God's righteousness that saves us, not our own (chaps. 40–55).

But Isaiah said, as does the New Testament (e.g., Eph. 2:10), that God's intention is that we should live righteous lives here and now, in order that our lives would be a witness to the world that Yahweh is the only Savior. The prophet makes his point with a very strongly worded contrast: a foreigner or a eunuch who truly lived out the obligations of the covenant was much more pleasing to God than a pure-blooded Judean who lived as though God's requirements were optional. That contrast is displayed powerfully in the selections chosen for this week, passages that begin and end this final section of the book of Isaiah.

ONE

Keep Justice; Do Righteousness

Isaiah 56:1–5 *Thus says the LORD: Maintain justice, and do what is right, for soon my salvation will come, and my deliverance be revealed.*

²Happy is the mortal who does this, the one who holds it fast, who keeps the sabbath, not profaning it, and refrains from doing any evil.

³Do not let the foreigner joined to the LORD say, "The LORD will surely separate me from his people"; and do not let the eunuch say, "I am just a dry tree." ⁴For thus says the LORD: To the eunuchs who keep my sabbaths, who choose the things that please me and hold fast my covenant, ⁵I will give, in my house and within my walls, a monument and a name better than sons and daughters; I will give them an everlasting name that shall not be cut off.

Understanding the Word. Throughout chapters 1–39 "justice" and "righteousness" are used as synonyms to talk about God's expectations for the way his people should live. But in chapters 40–55 the synonym for "righteousness" is "salvation." This is because in those chapters it is God's righteousness shown by keeping his promises to his people that is in focus. Thus, as I have noted, it would be very easy for the people to conclude that since salvation was all of grace, it was unimportant whether they were righteous or not (especially since they seemed unable to be so anyway).

But in the first part of the first verse of chapter 56, for the first time in more than fifteen chapters, Isaiah called on the people to keep justice and do righteousness, signaling that the requirement for righteous living has not been set aside. Then, in verses 2–8, he amplified this demand with two very shocking examples of what he was talking about. In short, the expectations have not changed.

But in the second part of verse 1 the prophet stated the reason we should keep justice and do righteousness: it is because Yahweh's salvation is at hand and *his* righteousness is about to be revealed in us. That is, God will empower us to live the kinds of righteous lives he calls us to live. Thus, in this last section of the book, Isaiah was combining his two treatments of righteousness: (1) we should live upright lives that reflect God's intended order for life (justice) because (2) he, in saving us, will impart his righteousness to us. In ourselves we cannot be righteous people. If we pride ourselves on being such, then that very pride is a sin against God. That theme will be explored in detail throughout this final segment of the book. But, by God's grace, no credit to us, we can live godly, Christlike lives.

The two examples used to justify the point being made in 56:1a were certainly very shocking to the Judeans, who were concerned to show that they really were descended from Abraham and were, thus, legitimate heirs of God's gracious promises. Those examples are the foreigner (introduced in verse 3 and expanded upon in verses 6–8) and the eunuch in verses 4–5. Both of these classes of people had been specifically excluded from worship in the book of Deuteronomy. Yet here they are being commended for their outstanding obedience in binding themselves to Yahweh. (See the commentary notes at the end of this week for a discussion of the reasons for the exclusion.) Clearly, Isaiah is attempting to make the point that his covenant promises are for *whoever will obey the covenant requirements*, while those who do *not* obey the requirements have no access to those promises regardless of their bloodlines. It is not about your pedigree, but about your relationship to God *as demonstrated* in the way you live your life.

That point could hardly be made more strongly than it is with reference to the eunuch (vv. 4–5). Here is a man who can have no children, someone whose "name" will die with him. He is a "dry tree," a dead stick. Yet God promises him a better kind of immortality than could be had in merely fathering a line of descendants. In God's house, his name will be remembered forever. Several commentators believe that this is one of the early intimations of the doctrine of resurrection that would come to full flower in the resurrection of Christ.

1. For us Christians, what would be the equivalent of the Judeans believing that their bloodline guaranteed them a place in God's favor regardless of the character of their lives?

2. If, as Christians, our righteous living does not earn us additional favor with God, why is it a requirement for us?

3. Why does obeying God's commandments apart from faith in Christ not earn us special favor with God?

TWO

My House Is a House of Prayer

Isaiah 56:6–8 *And the foreigners who join themselves to the* LORD, *to minister to him, to love the name of the* LORD, *and to be his servants, all who keep the sabbath, and do not profane it, and hold fast my covenant—⁷these I will bring to my holy mountain, and make them joyful in my house of prayer; their burnt offerings and their sacrifices will be accepted on my altar; for my house shall be called a house of prayer for all peoples. ⁸Thus says the Lord* GOD, *who gathers the outcasts of Israel, I will gather others to them besides those already gathered.*

Understanding the Word. The Old Testament speaks of two kinds of non-Israelite people. There is the "stranger" and the "foreigner." The stranger (*ger* in Hebrew) is a non-Israelite who had settled in Israelite territory. Although they did not have to practice Israelite religion, they could not practice pagan religion. But they could become naturalized if they chose to worship Yahweh and accepted the demands of his covenant (such as circumcision). Ruth is an example of such a person.

The foreigner (*nokri, neker* in Hebrew) was a non-Israelite who had no intention of forsaking his or her pagan religion. Such a person could travel through the land, and the Hebrews could have business relations with them, but neither they nor their children could have any part in Israelite life. It is such persons as these with whom the Israelites were forbidden to intermarry (Deut. 7:3–4).

Yet, it is the son of a foreigner (v. 3 NKJV) who is specifically commended here for binding himself to Yahweh so as to serve him. What was the prophet saying? He was clearly saying what this book has been about at least since chapter 2: Yahweh's salvation is not merely for his chosen people, Abraham's descendants. It is for the world. Abraham and his descendants were not chosen so they could hug their chosenness to themselves, but so that the world could "know" Yahweh in the fullest sense of that word. Yahweh's house is "a house of prayer for all [nations]" (v. 7), and he will not be content merely to "gather" the Judean exiles home, but there are still others that are on his heart (v. 8).

Jesus made the same point in a powerful way when he spoke of people coming from all directions to feast in the kingdom of God and that some who had been first would be last and vice versa (Luke 13:30). He made the point even more dramatically when he drove from the temple those who were raking in huge profits changing the money of those worshippers from other countries, and he quoted Isaiah 56:7 in the process (Matt. 21:12–13).

Thus, the issue is not what a person's parentage may have been, but what their relationship is to the God of the Bible. Any person could renounce the gods of their parents, as difficult as such a move would have been in that culture, and enter into the covenant with Yahweh. If they did that, and the quality of the life, their walk, demonstrated the reality of their choice, then they could live in the light of God's smile.

Notice the order of the statements in verse 6: join themselves, minister, love the name, be his servants, keep the Sabbath, hold fast the covenant (these last also in v. 4). The first four are a synonymous pair beginning with relationship and moving to service. The question is whether I want to belong to Yahweh, and am passionate that he be known rightly in the world. If so, my greatest desire will be to serve him. The truth of that desire will be shown in the details of my life.

Keeping the Sabbath came to be the heading under which all the rest of the specific commands of the covenant were encapsulated. Obviously, a merely mechanical keeping of the Sabbath proved nothing about one's relationship with Yahweh. On the other hand, if I am not willing to do even that as an expression of my love for him, what does that say about the rest of my obedience?

1. What is the line between a foreigner and a stranger? Why do you think Isaiah used the term "foreigner" and not "stranger" for his example?

2. Would permitting a local Buddhist group to use our church for worship be fulfilling the admonition, "My house shall be called a house of prayer for all peoples"? Why not? What is the intent of the statement?

3. Practically speaking, what does it mean for a Christian to hold fast to the covenant?

THREE

Blind Watchmen

Isaiah 56:9–57:2 *All you wild animals, all you wild animals in the forest, come to devour!* ¹⁰*Israel's sentinels are blind, they are all without knowledge; they are all silent dogs that cannot bark; dreaming, lying down, loving to slumber.* ¹¹*The dogs have a mighty appetite; they never have enough. The shepherds also have no understanding; they have all turned to their own way, to their own gain, one and all.* ¹²"*Come," they say, "let us get wine; let us fill ourselves with strong drink. And tomorrow will be like today, great beyond measure."*

⁵⁷:¹*The righteous perish, and no one takes it to heart; the devout are taken away, while no one understands. For the righteous are taken away from calamity,* ²*and they enter into peace; those who walk uprightly will rest on their couches.*

Understanding the Word. Rather like the sudden shifts found in chapters 1–5, the perspective of this passage and much of what follows through 59:15a is strikingly different from 56:1–8. Instead of the righteous foreigners and eunuchs of those verses, we are introduced to an Israel where the leadership is blind and the righteous disappear without the society's even noticing.

The condemnation of the leadership is strikingly similar to that found earlier in the book (see especially chapter 28). Likewise, later on, the condemnation of the people (57:3ff.) seems more reflective of pre-exilic times than post-exilic ones. Taken together, this may suggest that the pre-exilic author is speaking of the conditions of that future time in language that is reflective of his own time. At any rate, the point here is that the leaders who are supposed to be on guard for anything that will threaten the community's life have been blinded by their own self-interests. As a result, the flock is ripe for destruction. Mirroring his call for the wild animals to come and destroy the vineyard in chapter 5, here the prophet calls for the wild animals to come and devour the flock, since the leaders, described both as watchmen and watchdogs, have failed in their duties.

The failure is described on two levels. On the one hand the sentinels are either blind or asleep (v. 10). They are not conscious of the danger, and are not alert to its possibility. They lack knowledge (v. 10) and understanding (v. 11). They should recognize the danger of relying on one's religious birthright while neglecting to cultivate a truly righteous character of living. But they do not do this. Why not? It is because of the second level of failure. Why are the dogs asleep? It is because they have gratified their huge appetites and are sleeping it off. Why are the watchmen blind? It is because they have only two interests: "their own way" and "their own gain" (v. 11). They are so absorbed in their own self-interests that they can see nothing else. If they loved the name Yahweh and lived to serve him, then they would recognize what was happening among their people and where their attitudes were going to lead in the future. But these leaders can see nothing but the present, and the continuing fulfillment of their own desires (v. 12).

One of the things the leaders are blind to is the disappearance of the righteous from among their midst. Perhaps this is a reference to an older generation, perhaps the first generation of returnees, the old fogies who were so narrow and hidebound, whose passing off the scene is a relief to their children who have more progressive attitudes. But no one realizes what a cost their disappearance will entail. With their removal, some of the impediments to more rapid degeneration will be removed. Thus, in fact, they are actually being delivered from the troubles that those who remain will bring down upon themselves through their growing disobedience.

1. Using this passage as an opposite, what would be some of the characteristics of a good leader?

2. What similarities do you see between the conditions described here and some of the conditions in our own society?

3. Think of some of the righteous whom you have known who have died recently. Granting that all of us have failures and weaknesses, what are some of the qualities of those people that you would like to emulate in your own life and be sure do not disappear from the earth?

FOUR

Yahweh Will Execute Judgment

Isaiah 66:14–17 *You shall see, and your heart shall rejoice; your bodies shall flourish like the grass; and it shall be known that the hand of the LORD is with his servants, and his indignation is against his enemies. ¹⁵For the LORD will come in fire, and his chariots like the whirlwind, to pay back his anger in fury, and his rebuke in flames of fire. ¹⁶For by fire will the LORD execute judgment, and by his sword, on all flesh; and those slain by the LORD shall be many.*

¹⁷Those who sanctify and purify themselves to go into the gardens, following the one in the center, eating the flesh of pigs, vermin, and rodents, shall come to an end together, says the LORD.

Understanding the Word. Here we come to the parallel sections at the other end of the division comprised by chapters 56–66. The final unit (verses 18–24) parallels 56:1–8, and this one parallels the one we just looked at (56:9–57:2). When I say "parallels," I don't mean that the sections are mirror images of each other, but only that they reflect the same overall thought. So here, the point is like that of the previous passage: the righteous servants of God will be blessed (14a [like 57:1–2]), but his enemies will be punished (14b–17 [like 56:9–12]).

Verses 15 and 16 express an idea that is very uncomfortable for most of us. We like to dwell on the love of God. And that is as it should be. God *is* love; that is his very nature. However, we want to dispense with the corollary. Love is not a dispassionate, generalized benevolence. It is a positive passion that burns with a desire for the very best for the beloved. But when that passion is not merely rejected, but spurned, there is another side to the flame of love. It is this other side that we do not like to think about. But the truth is that we cannot have only one side of the coin. Notice that the metaphor of fire appears three times in these two verses. Throughout the Bible, fire is used as a metaphor for God, from the burning bush of Exodus 3 to the tongues of fire resting on the heads of the disciples in Acts 2. The metaphor is very apt. If fire is used in keeping with its own character and nature, and in the light of our character and nature, it will be a great blessing. But if we refuse to take account of those two differing natures and insist on using fire any way *we* wish, that tremendous power to bless will become a terrible, swift "sword" of destruction. On the one hand, God is not a petty tyrant who says, "If you dare to offend me, I will smash you." But on the other, he *is* the Sovereign of the universe and refusal to admit the nature of reality as he has made it can only have terrible consequences.

But what is the character of Yahweh's enemies, as it is defined in verse 17? Here the prophet is continuing in the sarcastic tone that he has used several times throughout the division to describe those who are proud of their religious purity while neglecting the relational behaviors that are meant to characterize those in covenant with God. It is highly unlikely that any observant Jew would think that they could make themselves holy by "eating the flesh of pigs, vermin, and rodents." So what is Isaiah wanting to convey? He is saying, just as he did in 1:10–15, but even more graphically, that religious behavior that is done without a corresponding quality of behavior is not merely useless, but actually takes us further from God, rather than closer. These people, like the later Pharisees, were very particular about performing rituals just exactly as the Torah laid them down, but since it was all self-serving, it did not really reflect love for God and neighbor.

1. If we do love God and our neighbor, what is the function of religious practices like church attendance, Bible reading, prayer, etc.?

2. Can you think of practical ways that we can avoid either of the following wrong attitudes: (1) God is a narrow-eyed judge waiting for us to make one misstep or (2) he is a kindly grandpa who lets us do whatever we want, and blesses us anyway?

3. What are some examples of self-serving religion in our day?

FIVE

I Am About to Come

Isaiah 66:18–24 *For I know their works and their thoughts, and I am coming to gather all nations and tongues; and they shall come and shall see my glory, ¹⁹and I will set a sign among them. From them I will send survivors to the nations, to Tarshish, Put, and Lud—which draw the bow—to Tubal and Javan, to the coastlands far away that have not heard of my fame or seen my glory; and they shall declare my glory among the nations. ²⁰They shall bring all your kindred from all the nations as an offering to the LORD, on horses, and in chariots, and in litters, and on mules, and on dromedaries, to my holy mountain Jerusalem, says the LORD, just as the Israelites bring a grain offering in a clean vessel to the house of the LORD. ²¹And I will also take some of them as priests and as Levites, says the LORD.*

²²For as the new heavens and the new earth, which I will make, shall remain before me, says the LORD; so shall your descendants and your name remain. ²³From new moon to new moon, and from sabbath to sabbath, all flesh shall come to worship before me, says the LORD.

²⁴And they shall go out and look at the dead bodies of the people who have rebelled against me; for their worm shall not die, their fire shall not be quenched, and they shall be an abhorrence to all flesh.

Understanding the Word. The division ends just as it began, with a discussion of people from the non-Jewish world—the nations being brought to the holy mountain, Jerusalem, to worship God. This is the goal of the entire book, and especially of this division. By the quality of his people's lives, a result of God's gracious coming to them (v. 18), the nations will be gathered in.

Three times it is said here that the focus will be upon seeing "the glory" of God (vv. 18–19). This is not merely a bright cloud; it is his reality, his significance. There is an air of solidity, of weightiness about this concept. It is powerfully expressed in Jesus' Last Supper discourse as recorded in the Gospel of John. Jesus asked that God would glorify him in the last hour so that he could finish his task of glorifying God on earth by completing the work God had given him (17:1–5). That is to say, the glory of God is that self-denying love which has been most truly displayed on the cross of Christ. We do not normally think of the excruciating death of a criminal as being a means of displaying divine glory, but that is precisely what Jesus was talking about. The glory that the nations come to Jerusalem to see is the glory of the God who dies for his people. (For a discussion of the regions and nations mentioned in verse 19, see the commentary notes at the end of the week.)

As the nations come streaming to Jerusalem, they will bring the scattered people of Israel with them (vv. 20, 22). It is hard not to think of what has happened in modern times, as the Jewish people have returned to their homeland after more than a thousand years of exile. It is said that they will be brought as though in offering to God (v. 20), and in many ways the state of Israel exists today in part because of the guilt of the Western nations over the Holocaust, which is a Latin term for the whole burnt offering.

The final verse, verse 24, is a typical feature of the book of Isaiah. Again and again, when some glorious promise of the future is made, the prophet bluntly calls us back to face present facts. So here, the promise that representatives of all the nations will come to God should not be taken to mean that *all* people will come to him. Grace will never remove from us the dignity of free will. Those who come to him will freely choose to do so. But there will be those who freely choose *not* to do so, persons who choose to live in rebellion against both the power and the grace of the I AM. But to do so is to cut oneself off from light and life and hope.

1. In what way is the cross glorious?

2. Why does God not simply declare everyone's sins forgiven?

3. What is the appropriate attitude of Christians toward the Jewish people?

COMMENTARY NOTES

i. It is not appropriate to call the people of Israel "Jews" before the return from the Babylonian exile, and, even then, it is problematic to use this term to describe them. The reason is that "Jew" is a development of the term *Jehudi*, which refers to someone from the Persian province of Yehud, Judah, and even more so, someone from the Roman province of Judea.

What we today know as Judaism, or the Jewish religion, is actually a descendant of Pharisaism. In Jesus' time, there were a large number of differing approaches to Old Testament interpretation, of which Pharisaism was one. In the end, this particular interpretation won out.

Thus, the Old Testament was not written by the Jews and it is not a Jewish book. There were no Jews before the return from exile in 598 BC, and the Jewish religion only came into existence at roughly the same time that Christianity did. Christianity and Judaism are both interpretations of the Hebrew Bible, the Old Testament. Thus, it is better to refer to God's people in the Old Testament either as "the Hebrews" or "the Israelites."

ii. Why were foreigners and eunuchs explicitly forbidden from participating in Israelite worship by the book of Deuteronomy, and why did Isaiah explicitly include them as being better examples of faithfulness than the pure-bred Judeans?

The answer is to be found in progressive revelation. This is not to say that the earlier statement is wrong and the later one right. Rather, it is to say that when one is teaching a child, one may make certain absolutistic kinds of statements that will need to be radically modified when the child grows older.

In this case, God was needing to deal with a people that had just spent four hundred years in one of the most religiously pluralistic cultures the world has ever known—ancient Egypt.

Much that they had learned in that environment was positively wrong. One example is that instead of there being many gods, there is only one God. (For evidence of their worship of idols, see Leviticus 17:7; Joshua 24:14; and Ezekiel 20:6–9.) And this is only one example; there were many other areas in which ancient, and wrong, understandings had to be radically expunged.

So, the foreigner, someone who by definition did not want to become a part of the Israelite covenant, and did not intend to renounce his or her religion, could not participate in Israelite life. If they did, there was a strong chance that their example would lead the Israelites away from their tenuous hold on their new faith.

Likewise, it was important to show that God alone had made the world as it is, and that we cannot mutilate ourselves in any way, whether in a mistaken idea that it would influence him in some way, or out of a desire to remake ourselves in some way that we wished (for whatever reason).

These and other examples were enforced in absolutistic ways to make the essential points for new believers. But people of more mature faith could understand that if a foreigner really did wish to renounce their pagan religion and embrace the Israelite one, there was no reason why they could not. And if self-mutilation was still forbidden, the person who had been mutilated by someone else, or was perhaps born in that condition, was not incapable of deep and genuine faith.

Isaiah used these two extreme examples to try to drive home his point. If representatives of these two groups of people, who had historically been forbidden to participate, demonstrated by their lives that they did, indeed, serve Yahweh, they were more acceptable to him than Judeans who had a long pure bloodline and were depending on that for their divine acceptance while living lives that were essentially pagan.

iii. It is significant that not only in 56:1–8 and 66:23, but elsewhere in this division of the book, Sabbath-keeping is made the sign of faithful acceptance of all the covenant requirements for holy living. This is somewhat surprising in the context, because a great deal of religious performance, under which heading Sabbath-keeping tends to be treated in the New Testament, comes in for scornful rejection here.

Perhaps the difference between Sabbath-keeping and the other rituals, especially sacrifices, is that it is more difficult to keep Sabbath in a self-serving way than it is to offer sacrifices. In fact, if one truly stops daily work on the Sabbath, giving one's servant and animals the day off, it may well be contrary to self-serving in that it may deprive one of both income and production.

Thus, it seems probable that for this reason Sabbath was being neglected while other ritual performance was being carried out. At any rate, Isaiah never condemns people for keeping the Sabbath as a way of trying to manipulate God. Rather, he seems to call on his hearers to practice it more faithfully as a concrete sign of their trust in God to provide for them.

iv. The worldwide inclusiveness of God's call is expressed in the particular regions and nations named in 66:19. Tarshish is at the western end of the Mediterranean Sea, the very west end of the known world at that time. Put is Libya, on the south side of the sea, while Lud (Lydia) is on the north side in what is now Turkey. Javan is Greece to the northwest, and Tubal is the Caucasus region to the north. Perhaps no eastern region is mentioned because the east represents the past, and these promises are aimed at the future, which in the Israelite mind was to the west.

WEEK ONE

GATHERING DISCUSSION OUTLINE

A. Open session in prayer.

B. View video for this week's readings.

C. What general impressions and thoughts do you have after considering the video and reading the daily writings on these Scriptures?

D. Discuss questions selected from the daily readings.

1. **KEY OBSERVATION:** Christian faith should result in transformed behavior.

   DISCUSSION QUESTION: For us Christians, what would be the equivalent of the Judeans believing that their bloodline guaranteed them a place in God's favor regardless of the character of their lives?

2. **KEY OBSERVATION:** God intends that no one should be excluded from worshipping him. However, persons should worship him according to his requirements, in ways that are in keeping with his unique nature.

   DISCUSSION QUESTION: Would permitting a local Buddhist group to use our church for worship be fulfilling the admonition, "My house shall be called a house of prayer for all peoples"? Why not? What is the intent of the statement?

3. **KEY OBSERVATION:** Good leadership is essential to both the survival and the growth of a group or organization.

DISCUSSION QUESTION: Using Isaiah 56:9–57:2 as an opposite, what would be some of the characteristics of a good leader?

4. **KEY OBSERVATION:** If we are to live healthy, productive Christian lives, it is important that we have a right understanding of God.

   DISCUSSION QUESTION: Can you think of practical ways that we can avoid either of the wrong attitudes: (1) God is a narrow-eyed judge waiting for us to make one misstep or (2) he is a kindly grandpa who lets us do whatever we want, and blesses us anyway?

5. **KEY OBSERVATION:** God's expressed desire is that the whole world should "see his glory." But Jesus seems to say his death on the cross will glorify God.

   DISCUSSION QUESTION: In what way is the cross glorious?

E. What facts and information presented in the commentary portion of the lesson help you understand the weekly Scripture?

F. Close session with prayer.

WEEK TWO

Isaiah 57:3–21; 65:1–10

Judgment and Hope

INTRODUCTION

In the material below we find Isaiah continuing his pronouncements against those who claim to belong to God, but whose behavior does not support that claim. As in the previous lesson, his language seems excessive to us. However, when we look at Jesus' words to the Pharisees (e.g., Matt. 23:27), we see a similar level of passion and hyperbole. We, in modern Western Protestant culture, perhaps tend to say less than we really feel, whereas in the Mediterranean culture, the opposite seems to be the case.

At any rate, while the people might not actually have been engaging in the behaviors described here (as noted in the previous lesson, it seems highly unlikely that a Judean, eating unclean food, would thereby consider himself more holy than someone else [as in 65:4–5]), Isaiah seems to be saying that they might as well be doing those things, given their attitudes and behaviors. This is particularly relevant to us: we do not worship idols, nor visit ritual prostitutes, nor sacrifice our children to idols/gods, so apparently Isaiah's words have nothing to do with us. But, in fact, for all too many professing Christians, we are claiming that we are the people of God, while our behaviors actually show that we are ruled by covetousness, by the desire for pleasure, and by pride, and that all too frequently we are sacrificing our children on those very altars.

But for us, as well as for the ancient Judeans, God has a word of hope. This is a characteristic of the book: destruction is never God's intended last word. If Isaiah was led to pronounce judgment, it was always in the hope that the pronouncements would bring the hearers to the point of confession and repentance so that Yahweh could pronounce words of restoration. The irony in the ancient situation was that it appears this material was written especially for those who had been "restored" from Babylon. What Isaiah was saying was that a change in physical location is not true restoration. Restoration must be restoration of the character of God in us; anything less is a miscarriage of the divine purpose in creation.

ONE

Children of a Sorceress

Isaiah 57:3–7 *But as for you, come here, you children of a sorceress, you offspring of an adulterer and a whore. ⁴Whom are you mocking? Against whom do you open your mouth wide and stick out your tongue? Are you not children of transgression, the offspring of deceit—⁵you that burn with lust among the oaks, under every green tree; you that slaughter your children in the valleys, under the clefts of the rocks? ⁶Among the smooth stones of the valley is your portion; they, they, are your lot; to them you have poured out a drink offering, you have brought a grain offering. Shall I be appeased for these things? ⁷Upon a high and lofty mountain you have set your bed, and there you went up to offer sacrifice.*

Understanding the Word. The opening "But as for you" draws an explicit contrast between the addressees here and "the righteous" who were passing from the scene as discussed in 57:1–2. These people, who would proudly describe themselves as "children of Israel," whose birthright would make them acceptable to God apart from their behavior, are really children of a prostitute sorceress, said Isaiah. It is possible he had in mind the ancient Near Eastern goddess of passion, named variously Inanna, Ishtar, Isis, Anat, Asherah, Aphrodite, and Venus, among others. That is, their behavior showed who their true ancestress was. They were enslaved to passion and desire.

The prophet did not tell us at whom the mockery in verse 4 was directed. Perhaps it was at those foreigners and eunuchs mentioned in chapter 56, people whom the well-bred Judeans who were living in sin considered to have no right to be in the community. It might also be people of the lower classes who were arguing that behavior is important. Perhaps the proud religionists were accusing them of being legalists. While gestures of mockery vary among cultures, it is interesting that in a wide number of cultures, including our own, sticking out the tongue is a common sign of derision and contempt.

Throughout the prophetic literature, the actions of worshipping the fertility gods of the pagan neighbors are referred to in similar language as that found in verse 5. (See the commentary section at the end of the week for further discussion.) The fertility of field and home were of paramount concern. If one did not have crops, animals, and children, life was both bleak and short. So it was a very comforting feeling to believe that one could have some positive control over the life forces of the cosmos, as opposed to the rather frightening feeling of having to surrender that control and simply treat one's neighbor rightly and trust Yahweh to supply these basic needs. The irony, of course, is that those fertility gods demanded that you sacrifice some of the very children that they had supposedly given you, something Yahweh never demanded.

We get a glimpse of the possible double entendre in Isaiah's words in verse 6. That verse suggests that when people bring offerings to Yahweh, hoping to gain his forgiveness, they are really sacrificing to "the smooth stones of the valley," that is, the idols. They think they are sacrificing to Yahweh, but because of the disconnect between their lives and their profession, they are, in effect, sacrificing to idols and accomplishing nothing except creating further distance between themselves and him.

1. What kinds of attitudes and behaviors make our religious behavior of no value?

2. Where is the line between trusting God for our needs, and using our own resources and abilities to manipulate the world to supply our needs?

3. How are we tempted to ridicule our brothers and sisters in the faith who we think are beneath us?

TWO

You Have Uncovered Your Bed

Isaiah 57:8–13 *Behind the door and the doorpost you have set up your symbol; for, in deserting me, you have uncovered your bed, you have gone up to it, you* *have made it wide; and you have made a bargain for yourself with them, you have loved their bed, you have gazed on their nakedness.* ⁹*You journeyed to Molech with oil, and multiplied your perfumes; you sent your envoys far away, and sent down even to Sheol.* ¹⁰*You grew weary from your many wanderings, but you did not say, "It is useless." You found your desire rekindled, and so you did not weaken.*

¹¹*Whom did you dread and fear so that you lied, and did not remember me or give me a thought? Have I not kept silent and closed my eyes, and so you do not fear me?* ¹²*I will concede your righteousness and your works, but they will not help you.* ¹³*When you cry out, let your collection of idols deliver you! The wind will carry them off, a breath will take them away. But whoever takes refuge in me shall possess the land and inherit my holy mountain.*

Understanding the Word. This paragraph uses heavily figurative language to speak of a second kind of behavior on which the prophets pronounced judgment. This is reliance on pagan nations for protection. As with the idols, the imagery is sexual. To make an alliance with such a nation is to desert your true husband, Yahweh, and get in bed with some other man (see Ezekiel 23:12–21).

The use of such imagery for both the worship of idols and alliances with pagan nations tells us something important about the nature of the covenant between Yahweh and his people, as he sees it. The pattern of the covenant at Sinai is very clearly that of a covenant between a great king and a subject people. That is, it is political, or governmental, in nature. But it is clear from the language here and in virtually all the other prophets, that Yahweh's understanding of his relationship with us goes far beyond this. From his point of view, the relationship is primarily nuptial, not governmental, in nature. While he is our king, the way he really sees himself is as our husband.

What is the difference between those two types of relationships? The relationship to a king is primarily formal and official. It involves respect and honor. In that setting we obey the king's commands because we must; he is in a position of power that we have officially recognized. Thus, to worship some other god than he is to break a commitment, to commit an act of rebellion. Likewise, to turn to some nation for support or protection is an act of untrust; we do not believe the king can give us these things.

But a relationship with a husband is personal. It involves not merely giving him a formal commitment, but much more, our very selves. Now we do what he wishes for love, not coercion. Now, to worship another god is to break a love-vow, to care nothing for the feelings of our husband. In the same way, to look to another nation is tantamount to saying, "Husband, you are inadequate, and I don't really need you." Understanding our relationship with Yahweh in this way puts his anger in a new light. The king, whose covenant has been violated, may react with rage because his honor has been defaced by such rebellion. But, in the act of adultery, we have trampled on the very person of our husband who has given us himself. We have said, "You are of no worth to me," and in acting that out, we are actually destroying ourselves. The anger of Yahweh is the anger of a broken heart.

1. Think of some ways in which thinking of God as husband instead of king changes how we understand our relationship with him.

2. In our relationship with God, what is the equivalent of trusting foreign nations?

3. How is sinning against God like committing adultery?

THREE

A Nation That Did Not Call on My Name

Isaiah 65:1–7 *I was ready to be sought out by those who did not ask, to be found by those who did not seek me. I said, "Here I am, here I am," to a nation that did not call on my name. ²I held out my hands all day long to a rebellious people, who walk in a way that is not good, following their own devices; ³a people who provoke me to my face continually, sacrificing in gardens and offering incense on bricks; ⁴who sit inside tombs, and spend the night in secret places; who eat swine's flesh, with broth of abominable things in their vessels; ⁵who say, "Keep to yourself, do not come near me, for I am too holy for you." These are a smoke in my nostrils, a fire that burns all day long. ⁶See, it is written before me: I will not keep silent, but I will repay; I will indeed repay into their laps ⁷their iniquities and their ancestors' iniquities together, says the LORD; because they offered incense on the mountains and reviled me on the hills, I will measure into their laps full payment for their actions.*

Understanding the Word. Here we are again looking at a parallel passage on the other side of the climactic central section of the book of Isaiah. Both 56:9–59:15a and 63:7–65:16 speak of the failure of the proudly religious people to live truly godly lives. We have looked at the opening part of the first, and here we look at the beginning of the final part from the second. Like the first, it offers a graphic picture of people who probably think that they are worshipping God when, in fact, what they are doing is a terrible offense to him. They are "a smoke in [his] nostrils" (v. 5). That language is probably an intentional contrast with the frequent description of sacrifices as creating "a pleasing odor" in God's nostrils (e.g., Gen. 8:21; Exod. 29:18).

Once again, the language that Isaiah used is deeply ironic. The people were sure that by doing all kinds of religious things they were seeking God, and calling on his name. In fact, they were not (v. 1). At the same time, God was stretching out his hands to them (v. 2), wanting to gather them in. We think of Jesus' words as he looked out over Jerusalem, "How often have I desired to gather your children together as a hen gathers her brood under her wings, and you were not willing!" (Matt. 23:37). The people wanted God on their terms, not on his. What was the problem? They were trusting in their own devices. That is, they thought they knew how to manipulate God, to placate him, and get what they wanted from him. They did not remember the words of God through Samuel, "Has the LORD as great delight in burnt offerings and sacrifices, as in obedience to the voice of the LORD? Surely, to obey is better than sacrifice, and to heed than the fat of rams" (1 Sam. 15:22).

The practices described in verses 3 and 4 were probably all familiar to the people of Isaiah's day as things their pagan neighbors did, and which the Judeans would all reject. But, as in the first part of the parallelism, the prophet said that those kinds of things were what they were really doing, in effect.

Verse 5 suggests one possibility for what is going wrong in the Judean community: they were seeking to make themselves holy. This was the failure of the later Pharisees. Now, to be sure, holiness, the sharing of the character of God, is what we are to strive for. Leviticus 19:2 is very clear that we must be holy as God is holy (see also 1 Peter 1:15–16). But the problem comes when we make holiness our aim. *God* is our aim. If the whole motive of our lives is to love and please him, then holiness is the natural by-product; we will become like the One we love. But when we make our aim our holiness, then *we*, and *our achievements*, take center stage, and the loving, nuptial relationship with God, indeed, God himself, gets pushed to the sidelines. That may well be what was happening here.

1. What is it that prevents us from loving God with our whole hearts and, thus, becoming his holy people?

2. What is the danger in saying, "Holiness is not my aim"?

3. Why is pride a danger for people of faith?

FOUR

With Those Who Are Contrite

Isaiah 57:14–16 *It shall be said, "Build up, build up, prepare the way, remove every obstruction from my people's way." ¹⁵For thus says the high and lofty one who inhabits eternity, whose name is Holy: I dwell in the high and holy place, and also with those who are contrite and humble in spirit, to revive the spirit of the humble, and to revive the heart of the contrite. ¹⁶For I will not continually accuse, nor will I always be angry; for then the spirits would grow faint before me, even the souls that I have made.*

Isaiah 65:8–10 *Thus says the LORD: As the wine is found in the cluster, and they say, "Do not destroy it, for there is a blessing in it," so I will do for my servants' sake, and not destroy them all. ⁹I will bring forth descendants from Jacob, and from Judah inheritors of my mountains; my chosen shall inherit it, and my servants shall settle there. ¹⁰Sharon shall become a pasture for flocks, and the Valley of Achor a place for herds to lie down, for my people who have sought me.*

Understanding the Word. For today's reflection, we are looking at two parallel passages together. In both cases, these follow directly on the previous pronouncements of judgment. Together they draw a typical picture for this book: God's hope is that words of judgment will result in real change.

Isaiah 57:14 is reminiscent of 40:4–5. There, every obstruction was to be removed so that Yahweh could come to his people in their trouble. Here, the obstructions are to be removed so that the people can come to him. Why does he want this? Because although he is "the high and lofty one" (the same as in 6:1) he also wants to live with his people. The language of verse 15 is remarkable for its strong contrasts. First of all, in four different ways it stresses Yahweh's absolute otherness: he is high and lofty, he is eternal, he is holy, and he dwells "in the high and holy place." What is the reason for this stress? I suggest that the prophet is laying the foundation for what comes next. God does not condescend to lowly people because he is a low-level God. He does not dwell with humble people because he has no reason for pride. No, the miracle of our God is that although he is absolutely beyond us in every way, he still delights to fellowship with the lowest of us. Here is glory; here is hope; here is redemption. Although Yahweh has every reason for a pride that would brook his having nothing to do with anything in his world (Aristotle's "unmoved mover," see the commentary section), that is not the case at all.

What is the qualification for knowing the blessed presence of the high, holy, eternal One in our lives? It is contrition and humility. Those who are proud and self-righteous can never know his presence, because their pride and arrogance have shut the door on him. But those who know themselves to be broken and helpless, and are willing to take the place of a servant (65:8–9), throw open the door to the Presence. Or, to change the metaphor, discover themselves on a highway that leads straight into those transcendent arms (see 35:8, 10).

As with any lover, God does not enjoy accusation and destruction, even if it is only the natural consequence of the defiant road those he would love have chosen. As the old Communion ritual says, his "property is always to have mercy." If he can find the least glimmer of a reason to forgive and restore, he will. After all, he made us, and he made us for love, so if we can give him the least basis for lavishing that love upon us, he will.

1. Suppose someone says, "I am not a bad person. I have nothing I need to be contrite about." How would you respond to them?

2. If humility is not bad-mouthing yourself (and it is not), what is it? What is healthy humility?

3. What does the realization of God's absolute otherness from us mean for your conception of his love?

FIVE

I Will Heal Them

Isaiah 57:17–21 *Because of their wicked covetousness I was angry; I struck them, I hid and was angry; but they kept turning back to their own ways. ¹⁸I have seen their ways, but I will heal them; I will lead them and repay them with comfort, creating for their mourners the fruit of the lips. ¹⁹Peace, peace, to the far and the near, says the* LORD; *and I will heal them. ²⁰But the wicked are like the tossing sea that cannot keep still; its waters toss up mire and mud. ²¹There is no peace, says my God, for the wicked.*

Understanding the Word. In many ways, the entire human problem is summed up in the word "covetousness." It is not accidental that it is the last of the Ten Commandments. Some say that it is the last of the neighbor commandments, and there is certainly some truth to that claim, since the commandment speaks about coveting what belongs to your neighbor. However, I wonder if this last command does not capture all that the previous nine are about. For in the end it is our covetousness (or in another word, our greed) that dethrones God, and our covetousness that makes us lust after our neighbor's possessions, his spouse, and even his life. Wanting never has enough. What we long for, although we do not know it, is God. If we have him, then whatever he permits us to have is enough. If we do not have him, then the whole world is not enough.

It is covetousness that explains idolatry. We want gods that we can manipulate in order to gratify our desires. It is covetousness that explains war. We want what someone else has, and we multiply weapons so that we will be able to take what they have. It is covetousness that explains our great difficulty in trusting others, including God. If we trust them, maybe they won't give us what we want. In the end, unless we surrender our covetousness to God, it will become the means of our justifying the breaking of every one of the other commands.

On the other hand, if we have dared to trust God through Christ, we have learned that he is infinitely trustworthy. Knowing that while we were still sinners, he did all that was necessary to restore us to himself, we can dare to believe that he will supply everything we really need. Our wants are completely relative to our place in him. There is an old hymn called, "Little Is Much When God Is in It."

That is the thrust of this passage. Notice that although we, as humans, keep turning back to our covetous ways (v. 17), nevertheless Yahweh has provided healing for us (v. 18). That demonstrates his trustworthiness. When we dare to make the first step of faith, he provides encouragement (comfort) to go on in faith. And when we see the way in which he provides, the "mourning" over the past results of our failure to trust is turned to shouts of joy ("the fruit of the lips," v. 18).

But what is the greatest fruit of this growing walk of fellowship and faith? It is *shalom* (v. 19). I hesitate to use the word "peace" because, while it is not incorrect, it is rather anemic beside all that the Hebrew term connotes. *Shalom* means wholeness—wholeness in relationships, wholeness within oneself, wholeness with creation. We can have shalom with God, shalom with others, and shalom with ourselves. God can take *all* the fragments of our lives and put them together. That is *true* peace.

But again, as is so typical of the book of Isaiah, the author will not leave us basking in the wonder of what God can do for us without warning us that these results have to be appropriated, that this shalom is not for those who get along just fine without God (vv. 20–21). (To be wicked is to conduct your life as if there is no God. Thus, very nice people can be thoroughly wicked.) He will not allow us to bask in some warm, fuzzy glow that does not face reality. If we choose to live without God, shalom is an impossibility.

1. What is the key to being healed of covetousness?

2. What prevents the wicked from finding shalom?

3. What are some of the evidences of shalom in a person's life?

COMMENTARY NOTES

i. The kinds of idolatrous practices described in 57:5 were common in many parts of the ancient Near East. One of the prime concerns was to get and maintain fertility, whether of crops, or animals, or in one's home. This meant that sexuality and sexual practices held a very high place in the religious framework. It was important that the gods and goddesses be sexually active and that such activity be productive in the world of nature. The way to ensure this was through rituals involving sexual activity. As the worshippers engaged in sexual activity with priests and priestesses, so the gods did as well.

Related to this was the sacrifice of the firstborn of crops, animals, and children. It was necessary to sacrifice these in order to ensure that there would be more following. This was both a sign of gratitude to the deities for their blessings, but also to be powerfully effective in persuading the gods to give such blessings (see Joshua 6:26; 2 Kings 3:27). While the Israelites sacrificed the first of crops and animals, they were forbidden to sacrifice their children. These were thought to belong to God already (Ezek. 23:37), and to sacrifice them in order to manipulate God was a terrible sin.

There is some disagreement among scholars as to how frequent child sacrifice was in the ancient world and in Canaan in particular. The extensive child cemetery at Carthage (a Phoenician [Canaanite] colony) has led many to believe that it was very common. Others treat this evidence as being only limited to that place.

ii. The phrase "under every green tree" (57:5) occurs ten times in the Old Testament, always in the context of idolatry. In the dry and at least partially denuded landscape of Canaan, trees were symbolic of life and reproductive capacity. Thus, they became objects of worship. Trees, perhaps poplars, were associated with the worship of the fertility goddess Asherah (e.g., Deut. 16:21).

iii. It is not clear what the "symbol" on the doorpost (57:8) refers to. It seems likely that it was some sort of a hex sign intended to protect the dwellers in the house from demonic power. This is in contrast to the expectation that the people would have placed a box containing a portion of the Torah on their doorposts. This is a good example of superficial similarities and essential differences. The "mezuzah," or Scripture box, was superficially like the hex sign. But instead of something magical to ward off the demonic, it was a reminder that as we store God's Word in our hearts, and make it a practical reality in our lives, we are more than conquerors.

iv. There is a good deal of uncertainty regarding the god Molech (57:9). He is referred to in 1 Kings 11:7 as the god of the Ammonites; however, in every other reference to the god of the Ammonites, the name is Milcom (cf. 1 Kings 11:5). Since the consonants are the same in both forms (*mlk*), it is possible that the name was indeed Milcom, and that "Molech" is a mockery in which the vowels of *boshet* "shame" have been substituted. However, there is fairly good evidence in many parts of the ancient Near East for the existence of a god called "Malik" (Hebrew spelling would render this Molek) who was thought to be the king of the underworld. This might explain why all of the occurrences except 1 Kings 11:7 are in connection with child sacrifice (see especially Leviticus 20:2–5).

v. Sharon (65:10) refers to a portion of the coastal plain south of Mount Carmel, extending south to the Yarkon River. It was about ten miles wide east to west, and about thirty miles long north to south. Like all the coastal plain in ancient times, it tended to be somewhat swampy with lush vegetation. Thus, it is symbolic of good pastureland.

In contrast, the Valley of Achor was one of the barren wadis leading up from the Jordan Valley to the central ridge. It is chiefly associated with the stoning of Achan (Josh. 7:24). By associating it with Sharon, Isaiah seems to be connoting the extraordinary fertility that will characterize the land when the people truly trust him, and give up their idolatry.

v. On Day 4 I referred to Aristotle's "unmoved mover." This was the famous Greek philosopher's idea that if there was a creative force behind everything, a force that brought everything else into being and set it all into motion, then that force could not be affected by anything it created. If it was so affected, then it could not truly be the first cause of everything. The creatures would be causing changes in the creator, which is not logically possible.

While that may be true according to human logic, the Bible calmly asserts that Yahweh is truly personal and does respond to his creatures' actions. Whether that is explainable by human logic is beside the point; Yahweh far transcends our logic.

WEEK TWO

GATHERING DISCUSSION OUTLINE

A. Open session in prayer.

B. View video for this week's readings.

C. What general impressions and thoughts do you have after considering the video and reading the daily writings on these Scriptures?

D. Discuss questions selected from the daily readings.

    1. **KEY OBSERVATION:** It is important that we learn to trust God to supply our needs and not fall into the idolatrous practice of trying manipulate the world to supply those needs.

    DISCUSSION QUESTION: Where is the line between trusting God for our needs, and using our own resources and abilities to manipulate the world to supply our needs?

    2. **KEY OBSERVATION:** Our images of God often control the ways we think of him in ways we are not conscious of. Many view him only as a king.

    DISCUSSION QUESTION: Think of some ways in which thinking of God as husband instead of king changes how we understand our relationship with him.

    3. **KEY OBSERVATION:** We are called upon to love God with our whole heart and, thus, be transformed into his likeness.

DISCUSSION QUESTION: What is it that prevents us from loving God with our whole hearts and, thus, becoming his holy people?

4. **KEY OBSERVATION:** The only appropriate stance toward God is one of contrition and humility.

   DISCUSSION QUESTION: If humility is not bad-mouthing yourself (and it is not), what is it? What is healthy humility?

5. **KEY OBSERVATION:** In many ways covetousness is the root of all evil.

   DISCUSSION QUESTION: What is the key to being healed of covetousness?

E. What facts and information presented in the commentary portion of the lesson help you understand the weekly Scripture?

F. Close session with prayer.

"Let it begin in me"

WEEK THREE

Isaiah 58:1–59:15a

Righteousness Does Not Reach Us

INTRODUCTION

One of the issues that continues to divide Christians is regarding sin in a believer's life. It is very clear throughout the New Testament that sin, the thing that killed Jesus, should have no place among us (see especially Romans 6). Yet, for many, experience seems to say that it does. So how should we think about it? Should we fight against sin continually, even though it often seems to master us, expecting that after death, we will finally be free of its allure and power? Or should we, as seems increasingly to be the case among us, simply say that sin is an inescapable part of the human condition, and while we ought to avoid it wherever possible, we should simply live under the umbrella of God's grace and not worry too much about it?

The material that we are studying this week will have none of the latter position. Sin is something terrible, something to be abhorred. It blinds us to what is good and true, and it deludes us as to the real condition of our lives. If sin is present in the lives of God's people, that is wrong. It should not be that way. But, even more to the point, it does not *have* to be that way. Even in this passage, which is majoring on the failure of God's servants to manifest his character, there are clear statements that such a failure does not have to be the case; God can lead us out of the darkness of continuing sin into the light where our continual delight is in him, and our walk with him is above reproach.

In this regard, it is important to recognize that there are "sins" and "Sin," and the failure to distinguish between these two is at the heart of much that is wrong in the church today. Sins are the occasional falling short of all that is characteristic of God in his perfection. We must guard against such thoughts and actions, and when they occur must reject them and seek God's grace not to commit them again. But until we are glorified, we will be liable to them. But the real issue is Sin. This is an attitude; an expression of the unsurrendered will. It is the determination to have our own way whatever the cost. This is the attitude that, as the apostle Paul said, must be crucified (Rom. 6:6, 11). Until that happens, we cannot please God, no matter how we live, because we are living for ourselves, not him; we are living in Sin. On the other hand, when such a thorough death to our own way has occurred, and is then put into practice daily through the power of the Holy Spirit, we are living in Christ and will manifest his life wherever we are and in whatever we do.

ONE

As If They Were a Nation That Practiced Righteousness

Isaiah 58:1–5 *Shout out, do not hold back! Lift up your voice like a trumpet! Announce to my people their rebellion, to the house of Jacob their sins. ²Yet day after day they seek me and delight to know my ways, as if they were a nation that practiced righteousness and did not forsake the ordinance of their God; they ask of me righteous judgments, they delight to draw near to God. ³"Why do we fast, but you do not see? Why humble ourselves, but you do not notice?" Look, you serve your own interest on your fast day, and oppress all your workers. ⁴Look, you fast only to quarrel and to fight and to strike with a wicked fist. Such fasting as you do today will not make your voice heard on high. ⁵Is such the fast that I choose, a day to humble oneself? Is it to bow down the head like a bulrush, and to lie in sackcloth and ashes? Will you call this a fast, a day acceptable to the LORD?*

Understanding the Word. Here and in at least one other place in this part of the book of Isaiah (64:8–65:2), the prophet highlights the difference between appearance and reality in relation to God. This ought to touch the hearts of all of us. How easily we learn, from childhood on, to project the image that we think is expected of us. Nowhere is that more of a danger than in the realm of religion. Religion, the attempt to get blessing and avoid cursing from whatever powers we conceive to be running the world, depends so heavily on what the gods (and the humans in our group) think of us. But the fact is, and again, it is a fact we learn very early, that it is easier to manufacture appearances than it is to demonstrate reality.

That was the case with the Judeans. On the surface, they looked like very righteous people, people who were really seeking God. After all, they did the right things, like engaging in regular fasts. Surely "afflict[ing]" (v. 5 KJV) or "humbl[ing] oneself" (the Hebrew phrase that is often associated with fasting, NRSV) ought to show how determined they were to please God and ought to earn them some points in heaven.

But that was the very point Yahweh was trying to make through Isaiah: they were not being obedient in their religious performances, but rebellious! They were not engaging in this and other acts of worship of God's sake, but for their own. That point is made very clearly in verse 3: "you serve your own interest." Far from their life with God being an expression of the crucified will, their religion was only an attempt to get what they wanted for themselves to *fulfill* their own will. They did not get the point. They thought religious behavior gave them a pass to then treat other people just like they were treating God, as a means to their own ends. The disconnect was so deep that it did not occur to them that oppression, litigation, and violence might be displeasing to God.

1. Think of some instances in contemporary church life where there is a disconnect between appearances and reality.

2. How can you and I guard against such a disconnect in our own lives?

3. If fasting is not for the purpose of manipulating God, what is its purpose, and how can we be sure we fulfill that purpose?

TWO

The Fast That I Choose

Isaiah 58:6–10 *Is not this the fast that I choose: to loose the bonds of injustice, to undo the thongs of the yoke, to let the oppressed go free, and to break every yoke? [7]Is it not to share your bread with the hungry, and bring the homeless poor into your house; when you see the naked, to cover them, and not to hide yourself from your own kin? [8]Then your light shall break forth like the dawn, and your* *healing shall spring up quickly; your vindicator shall go before you, the glory of the LORD shall be your rear guard. ⁹Then you shall call, and the LORD will answer; you shall cry for help, and he will say, Here I am.*

If you remove the yoke from among you, the pointing of the finger, the speaking of evil, ¹⁰if you offer your food to the hungry and satisfy the needs of the afflicted, then your light shall rise in the darkness and your gloom be like the noonday.

Understanding the Word. God does not much care whether we stop eating or not, but he does care that we stop doing other things. Interestingly, all those other things have to do with other people. That is no accident. The surest evidence that we have allowed him to deliver us from self-interest is in the way we treat others. This is why Jesus made that dramatic (and from one point of view, unexpected) statement in the upper room: "By this everyone will know that you are my disciples, if you have love for one another" (John 13:35). If it had been left up to me, I am afraid I might have picked a lot of other evidence before I chose that one. But, in reality, if we have been tracking with God through the Bible, it should not come as a surprise. God is love, and he made us to lavish his love on us. But there is this about love: in order to receive more of it, we have to give away what we have already received. Thus, much of the covenant has to do with how we treat others, and especially those who cannot repay us. Loving God is inseparable from loving others (see 1 John 5:1–5).

While some of the examples cited here (such as not oppressing workers, or bringing the homeless into our homes) might not apply to us in our social setting today, it still might very well apply, and in any case the principle will always apply. I am a professor; how do I treat my students? Are they underlings whom I can treat as I wish? How do I relate to those who maintain the physical plant at my institution? Are they invisible to me, or are they real people worthy of gratitude and conversation? What about those who serve us in various capacities? Do we treat them as worthy of our consideration?

If we do not have direct contact with the poor and homeless, are we making an effort to support those who do have that contact? It is to those who cannot repay us that we must be most generous, because that is what Jesus Christ has done for us. We can never repay him, but we can show our gratitude to all those around us no matter the situation. Isaiah's words here remind us of those of Jesus when he called upon his followers to visit the sick and imprisoned, to clothe the naked and feed the hungry (Matt. 25:35–40), and it is very possible that he had this passage in mind.

Light breaking forth in verse 8 is significant because it presages that great theme in chapter 60. When God's people manifest his character in the dark world, then the peoples of earth, as when the sun rises, will be able to see reality. But when we do not manifest his character then not only are we in darkness (as in 59:9–15a), but so is the world. Ironically, when we stop seeking his blessings and concentrate on replicating his love in reality (and not just in appearance), God is able to do what he wanted to but could not before: shower us with blessings (vv. 8–9)!

1. Why is the way we treat others the true evidence of our relationship with God?

2. Can you identify one concrete way in which you can minister to someone who cannot repay you?

3. If you fasted one meal a week, what could you do with the money from that meal?

THREE

You Shall Take Delight in the Lord

Isaiah 58:11–14 *The Lord will guide you continually, and satisfy your needs in parched places, and make your bones strong; and you shall be like a watered garden, like a spring of water, whose waters never fail. ¹²Your ancient ruins shall be rebuilt; you shall raise up the foundations of many generations; you shall be called the repairer of the breach, the restorer of streets to live in.*

¹³If you refrain from trampling the sabbath, from pursuing your own interests on my holy day; if you call the sabbath a delight and the holy day of the Lord honorable; if you honor it, not going your own ways, serving your own interests, or pursuing your own affairs; ¹⁴then you shall take delight in the Lord, and I will make you ride upon the heights of the earth; I will feed you with the heritage of your ancestor Jacob, for the mouth of the Lord has spoken.

Understanding the Word. At first glance these verses seem to go directly against what was said in the previous verses. There the people were engaging in a religious activity: fasting. And Yahweh, in effect, told them to stop because they were doing it for their own interests (i.e., trying to get him to bless them). Now it seems as though God is *wanting* them to engage in a religious activity: Sabbath-keeping. He seems to be saying that such behavior is a prerequisite to receiving his blessings (v. 11) and becoming a blessing to those around us (v. 12). What is going on?

The key appears in verse 13 in the twice-repeated phrase, "your own interests." That was the issue in fasting, wasn't it? They were fasting for their own interests, and here they are "trampling the sabbath" in order to pursue their own interests. The point is that, especially in an agrarian society, if you stop working on the Sabbath day, or if you permit your servants to stop working on that day, there will be a cost in lost income. This was not a case of people who were rigorously keeping every little detail of man-made Sabbath requirements (like the later Pharisees) in order to get God's blessings. Rather, they were treating that day just like any other, not as a holy day. Fasting was not very difficult, and did not really cost much, but Sabbath-keeping could be very costly, especially if, for instance, an unexpected storm came and destroyed the grain you would have harvested if you had worked on God's day. Keeping the Sabbath involved a level of trust in God, and a surrender of your own interests, that fasting did not begin to touch.

Thus, the central issue throughout this chapter is whether we will surrender our own self-interest to God in radical trust of him. Is our life consumed with pursuing our own interests, so that the way we pursue our religious activities is actually determined by that motive, rather than the love of God and others? If so, we will not be moved to ask what activity pleases God, but what is most likely to give us what we want, and that way leads to barrenness and disaster (see 1:29–31). But if we will, by the power of the Holy Spirit, abandon our selfishness, and learn to trust God in deep ways, we will become "like a watered garden" (v. 11), and the kind of reliable, constructive, encouraging people upon whom every church depends (v. 12).

1. How should the issue of self-interest enter into a discussion of our observance of the Sabbath today?

2. If our observance (or lack of observance) is an expression of self-interest, what should we do?

3. What are the proper reasons for engaging in religious activities?

FOUR
Your Iniquities Have Been Barriers

Isaiah 59:1–4, 7–8 *See, the Lord's hand is not too short to save, nor his ear too dull to hear. ²Rather, your iniquities have been barriers between you and your God, and your sins have hidden his face from you so that he does not hear. ³For your hands are defiled with blood, and your fingers with iniquity; your lips have spoken lies, your tongue mutters wickedness. ⁴No one brings suit justly, no one goes to law honestly; they rely on empty pleas, they speak lies, conceiving mischief and begetting iniquity. . . . ⁷Their feet run to evil, and they rush to shed innocent blood; their thoughts are thoughts of iniquity, desolation and destruction are in their highways. ⁸The way of peace they do not know, and there is no justice in their paths. Their roads they have made crooked; no one who walks in them knows peace.*

Understanding the Word. Here we seem to break into a dialogue. As in the parallel section (63:4–66:17), the people seem to have been asking God why he has not made them able to do his will and be empowered to live righteous lives. His response is that their "iniquities have been barriers" between them and himself (v. 2). That is, their continued sins make it more and more difficult for them to even hear God, let alone receive his empowerment.

All of this speaks of the importance of training children from earliest days to respond to God's voice. It is true that unless God draws a person to himself, he or she is incapable of coming to him. We cannot simply decide on our own that we will turn to God; our fear of him and our fear of losing control are simply too deeply ingrained in us. He has to draw us to him. But unlike what is taught in some segments of the church, that drawing is not irresistible. We can choose not to respond to his offer of grace, and when we do, it will be that much more difficult to hear his voice the next time he calls. This is why

36

deathbed conversions by persons who have lived their lives in defiance of God are so rare.

It is unfortunate that modern English no longer has a good equivalent for the Hebrew word *áwon*. The word has been translated as "iniquity" by the King James Version and its successors. But that word has almost completely disappeared from common English usage. It is unfortunate because the Hebrew word conveys a very important concept concerning sin. *Áwon* seems to express the objective reality of wrongdoing. We cannot say, "Oh, that was just a mistake, let's forget about it." No, when we do wrong, an irreducible fact comes into existence, one that must be dealt with, and, if possible, counteracted.

That is what Isaiah is speaking of here. "Iniquities"/"iniquity" occurs three times in the printed passage (vv. 2, 3, 7). The Judeans have done some things that have entered the record of life. Those things cry out for retribution. The scales of justice are far overbalanced, and God cannot simply ignore that fact. Likewise, because the Judeans have persisted in this wrongdoing (described here as extending all the way from lying to murder), they are increasingly deaf to God's offers of mercy, an offer that we Christians understand can be made because of the atoning death that Christ would suffer.

A final point needs to be made about the recurrence of words for roads and walking in verses 7 and 8. Notice "highways," "way," "paths," and "roads," as well as "feet run," "rush," and "walks." Throughout the book of Isaiah, these ideas are very prominent. Life is a progression, and one that becomes increasingly proscribed as we proceed through it. The paths we choose early on become almost unchangeable as we grow older. That had become true for the Judeans; they had chosen roads of self-serving, and those roads had now become deep ruts of lies, oppression, and violence.

1. Why is it that sinning once makes it easier to sin the next time we are tempted?

2. How should the understanding that sinning introduces a new fact into existence shape our thinking and responses about Sin and sins?

3. What does your path look like? Is God telling you that you need to turn in another direction?

FIVE

We Stumble at Noon

Isaiah 59:9–15a *Therefore justice is far from us, and righteousness does not reach us; we wait for light, and lo! there is darkness; and for brightness, but we walk in gloom. ¹⁰We grope like the blind along a wall, groping like those who have no eyes; we stumble at noon as in the twilight, among the vigorous as though we were dead. ¹¹We all growl like bears; like doves we moan mournfully. We wait for justice, but there is none; for salvation, but it is far from us. ¹²For our transgressions before you are many, and our sins testify against us. Our transgressions indeed are with us, and we know our iniquities: ¹³transgressing, and denying the LORD, and turning away from following our God, talking oppression and revolt, conceiving lying words and uttering them from the heart. ¹⁴Justice is turned back, and righteousness stands at a distance; for truth stumbles in the public square, and uprightness cannot enter. ¹⁵Truth is lacking, and whoever turns from evil is despoiled.*

Understanding the Word. This is certainly one of the grimmest passages in the Bible. Here the prophet enters into his people's experience, identifying with them in their despair over their inability to do what they know they should. Although the tone is darker than that of Romans 7, the point is much the same in both passages: something in us seems to prevent us from living the life of God.

There are several key concepts here. One is the pairing of justice and righteousness. In chapters 1–39, the terms are used together to speak of God's expectation for his people's lives. But they did not such lives and so ended up in exile. In chapters 40–55, which are addressed to the exiles, justice is what the Servant is going to bring into the world, while God's righteousness is his gracious deliverance of his people. If the book had ended at chapter 55, we might have believed that God no longer expected justice and righteousness of his people, however this last part of the book makes it clear that Yahweh's expectations have not changed. But now the question is highlighted: How can that expectation be realized, given the apparently complete inability of the people to live such lives?

Negatively speaking, the failure is described with the three words that most frequently define wrongdoing in the Old Testament: "sin," "iniquity," and "transgression." The first generally refers to any deviation from God's character and will, whether intentional or not. Iniquity speaks of the inescapable facticity of sin. The world has been altered because of something wrong that was thought, said, or done. Transgression refers to open and intentional rebellion, the most "in your face" of the three.

Another important concept here is darkness. In 1 John we read that God is light, and if a person's life does not correspond to God's life, they are in darkness (1:5–7). That is what the prophet understands on behalf of his people here. Light makes life possible, and where there is no light, there is no life. The way the people are living is the way of death, and it is so because the path they have chosen is not the one "following our God" (v. 13). They have denied Yahweh, and their mouths are filled with lies that emerge from the heart.

This introduces the final concept: truth. In the Old Testament, "truth" is used to describe a person who is true. That is, like Yahweh, he or she is utterly reliable. If they say they will do something, they will do it! You can trust such a person. They are not a slave to their own interests. Lies come straight out of that enslavement. It is fascinating that in life, lies and selfishness seem inseparable. From earliest childhood, that is the case. Truth transcends self-interest, and thus is often very costly, as the last verse of our passage points out. We are not talking about the person who is proud, because they always tell the truth (especially if it is costly to someone else). No, we are speaking of the person who is completely trustworthy because the interest of others is more important to them than their own (see Philippians 2:3–4).

1. What is the connection between self-interest and lying, injustice, rebellion, and oppression? Why is this so?

2. Reflect on the connection between sin and the metaphor of darkness. Why is it an appropriate metaphor?

3. Does this passage describe your life in any way? If so, what needs to happen to change that?

COMMENTARY NOTES

i. The Bible is somewhat ambivalent concerning the practice of fasting. The only two places where it is commanded are in connection with the Day of Atonement (Lev. 16:29, "deny yourselves") and in Joel 1:14 and 2:15, where the people are to repent of their sins and thus be delivered from the locust plagues (which are perhaps metaphorical for enemy armies). Otherwise, it is only reported that this was something the people did (e.g., Zech. 7:3), or that a ruler commanded (e.g., 2 Chron. 20:3). In several cases, it is said to have been a fruitless endeavor because it did not involve genuine repentance (Jer. 14:12; Zech. 7:5–6), or even a wrong one (as in the case of Naboth where it was a front for making false charges against him [1 Kings 21:9–10]).

In all cases, it was expected to be an act of contrition and repentance because of sin, so that God would forgive the person or persons and act favorably toward them. The danger lay in doing it without any real contrition or repentance, as here, but simply as a way of convincing God that the person or persons were really serious about whatever they were asking God to do. This is when fasting becomes manipulative.

ii. In 58:8, the New Revised Standard Version translates "your righteousness" as "your vindicator." (See also 62:2, where the same phrase is translated "your vindication," and 63:1, where "speaking in righteousness" is translated as "announcing vindication.") The reason for this is because in chapters 40–55, "righteousness" is frequently an attribute of Yahweh and is used to refer to his various acts of deliverance. The translators choose to understand the term in that way in certain places in this section as well, even when it does not explicitly refer to Yahweh. However, the context in this section is very different than that of 40–55. Whereas chapters 40–55 did not include any demand for righteous living, but only continuing faith in God's promises, this section does make such demands regularly and consistently. Thus, there is every reason to believe that when a passage speaks of "your righteousness" it is intending to speak of their righteous behavior, or, as the case may be, their unrighteous behavior. In 58:8 it seems very clear that when the people stop living in sinful ways (i.e., repent), then they will be healed of their sinning and their righteousness will be apparent to the watching world.

iii. It is important to remember that the Hebrew word *mishpat*, usually translated as "justice" or "judgment," connotes more than either of those English words does. It refers to God's divine order for life. One very significant element of that order is legal equity, or "justice," for all persons regardless of status or position because God values all persons equally. But if we limit *mishpat* merely to the conventional idea of justice in English, we miss much of the richness of the idea. When God's intended order for life is truly reigning in our life, when we are keeping *mishpat* (Isa. 56:1), then we do not merely give others their minimal legal due, but we actively seek their best; that is, we love them. We embody integrity in all our dealings with others; we can be counted on to do what is right in every circumstance; we will be completely reliable, etc. This is what is meant when Isaiah 42:1 says that the Servant will bring "justice to the nations," and why 59:15b says he was displeased "that there was no justice." He is lamenting the lack of legal equity in the society, but much more than that, God is lamenting the absence of his intended order for human life among his people.

iv. Given the importance of Sabbath-keeping in the Old Testament (e.g., one of the Ten Commandments, Exod. 20:8–11; Deut. 5:12–15, with extended treatments in both places), especially in the prophets, it is noteworthy that what is said of it in the New Testament is primarily negative. The majority of the references are found in the Gospels, and almost all of them are reporting how Jesus offended the religious leaders with his violation of the various traditional ways of honoring the Sabbath commandments. This is not to say that he disregarded the Sabbath (see Luke 4:16, 31; 6:6; 13:10), but only that he had no use for the extra strictures that the Jews had come to put on the observance.

Still, it is significant that not once does Jesus command his followers to keep the Sabbath. Neither does the apostle Paul. In fact, the only reference to the Sabbath in Paul's writings is found in Colossians 2:16, where he tells his followers not to allow anyone to judge them in regards to "new moons, or sabbaths." This in spite of the fact that he was clearly an observant Jew (e.g., Acts 13:14).

How should we understand these facts and what bearing should they have on us as Christians? There are two issues that should be taken into account. First, there is the importance of a day of rest and worship, a day when we, in effect, show that all our time belongs to God, and is received as a gift from him. By stopping any but necessary work, and coupling that with corporate worship, we are reminding ourselves and each other that God is the supplier of our needs and not us.

The second issue is that any kind of religious activity can easily become a means of manipulating God. When that happens, it is almost inevitable that external forms become very important. That is clearly what happened in Pharisaic Judaism. Sabbath-keeping, especially in a more urban environment, had become a means of procuring blessing, just as fasting had in Isaiah's day, and if the blessing was to be procured, then the keeping had to be of rigorous perfection. If not, the blessing device would not work. Here again, the principle has to be: the outward activity is a symbol of inward reality. It is not a device to obtain blessing, but an expression of gratitude for blessings already received, and of submissive trust for all that a good Father wishes to bestow upon us in days to come.

Some would say that if we are truly going to keep the commandment, then we should observe it on Saturday, the last day of the week, in obedience to the Old Testament commands. However, this overlooks a fundamental principle of Old Testament/New Testament interpretation. In the Old Testament, as is appropriate in a teaching situation, the practice and the principle are inseparable. One example is the sacrificial system. But it is the principle that is important. In the New Testament, the practice and the principle are regularly separated. Christ is our sacrifice, so the practice of sacrifice is superseded. So also in regards to Sabbath-keeping. The principle is that we should have a day of worship and rest. In the Old Testament, the practice commemorated the act of creation. In New Testament times, it came to be believed that the most appropriate time for worship and rest was on that day of the week when Jesus arose and the Holy Spirit was given, namely the day of redemption. So here, as elsewhere, the practice is the means of demonstrating the principle, which is the end.

v. If it is true, as was mentioned above in the context of 59:1–4, that we cannot repent unless God enables us to do so, then it seems that determinism becomes inescapable. In other words, if there are those who do repent and those who do not, it must be because God has chosen some whom he will enable to repent and others whom he will not. This was the position to which the great reformer John Calvin came, following the prior lead of Saint Augustine. Grace is given only to a few, and for those to whom it is given it is irresistible, and will inevitably bring them to final salvation.

The alternative proposed by a contemporary of Augustine named Pelagius denied Augustine's first premise. This was the conviction that humans are so deeply mired in what I have labeled Sin, that is, determination to have our own way, that they are unable to choose God's way. In Pelagius's view, there remains a spark of goodness in us that enables us to choose God if we so desire. The problem with this is that the Bible nowhere suggests it. Rather, it depicts us as being totally sinful (e.g., Gen. 6:5; and the catena of quotations in Rom. 3:9–18).

But there is another alternative, one suggested by John Wesley. He called it "prevenient grace," the grace that comes before. Looking at the clear biblical statements that, on the one hand, we are completely sinful and, on the other, that God does not will that any should perish (2 Pet. 3:9), and, "Let anyone who wishes take the water of life as a gift" (Rev. 22:17), Wesley proposed that God has graciously made available to all sinful persons the ability to turn away from their sins and to God. In this elegant way, Wesley showed how the two seemingly contradictory teachings of Scripture need not be contradictory at all.

WEEK THREE

GATHERING DISCUSSION OUTLINE

A. Open session in prayer.

B. View video for this week's readings.

C. What general impressions and thoughts do you have after considering the video and reading the daily writings on these Scriptures?

D. Discuss questions selected from the daily readings.

1. **KEY OBSERVATION:** It is a fact that appearances and reality do not always coincide. This is a particular danger in the church, where we claim to speak of divine realities.

   DISCUSSION QUESTION: Think of some instances in contemporary church life where there is a disconnect between appearances and reality.

2. **KEY OBSERVATION:** The Bible regularly makes the way we treat others the real indicator of what sort of relationship we have with God.

   DISCUSSION QUESTION: Why is the way we treat others the true evidence of our relationship with God?

3. **KEY OBSERVATION:** The central issue about Sabbath-keeping relates to whether doing so would serve one's self-interest or not.

   DISCUSSION QUESTION: How should the issue of self-interest enter into a discussion of our observance of the Sabbath today?

4. **KEY OBSERVATION:** To commit sin, whether by an act, or in a thought, is to introduce a new fact into existence. It alters the shape of reality.

   DISCUSSION QUESTION: How should the understanding that sinning introduces a new fact into existence shape our thinking and responses about Sin and sins?

5. **KEY OBSERVATION:** To live for the sake of self-interest is to choose the world of darkness: lying, injustice, rebellion, and oppression.

   DISCUSSION QUESTION: What is the connection between self-interest and lying, injustice, rebellion, and oppression? Why is this so?

E. What facts and information presented in the commentary portion of the lesson help you understand the weekly Scripture?

F. Close session with prayer.

Isaiah 63:7–64:12

You Are Our Father!
Will You Keep Silent?

INTRODUCTION

In the introduction to chapters 56–66, I presented the idea that this division of the book of Isaiah is arranged as a chiasm. That is, it is arranged as a pyramid with matching emphases on either side of the pyramid as the overall thought proceeded up to the central climax (61:1–3). One of these matching emphases is that the returnees from captivity in Babylon seem unable to live genuinely godly lives. The first expression of this idea is in 56:9–59:15a, which we have covered in the previous two weeks. Now we come to the parallel segment in 63:7–66:17. Here, there is a slightly different tone from 56:9ff. There, the predominant emphasis was on accusation. The prophet was accusing his people of pretending to be holy and religious when, in fact, their lives showed little evidence of Yahweh's presence. Here, although there is accusation (65:1–16; 66:1–4, 15–17), there is also a recurring plaintive note, as the prophet, speaking for the people (as in 59:1–15a), tried to understand what had gone wrong in the relationship between Israel and God, and how the glorious past relates to the all-too-inglorious present.

Memory is important in our walk with Yahweh. We need to remember what he has done for us in the past, how he forgave us and restored us, how he empowered us and led us. When we do this, we can be both convicted and encouraged. We can be convicted as we look back upon the zeal that characterized us as young Christians, and at the courageous faith we had (even if it was called "foolish" by some), as we dared to trust God to work in and through us. But we can also be encouraged when we remember the ways in which God kept his promises to us even when we may not have always kept ours to him.

But looking back may also be troubling, as it is in this instance. The prophet recognized that his people were far from where they once were with God. How could this have happened? he asked. And perhaps more frightening, Did it mean that God had given up on them? That was what terrified Ezra when he returned to Jerusalem in 458 BC, nearly eighty years after the first return, and found the people living sinful lives that were virtually indistinguishable from the lives of the unbelievers around them (Ezra 9:6–15). Yahweh had sent them into captivity on account of their sins. Then, with free grace he had brought them back home again. But there they were, eighty years later, doing the same things all over again! What would a just God do to them?

Similar thoughts go through this segment. But God firmly rejected any suggestion that he was the source of their problem. Instead, he insisted that the issue was a matter of their own wills. They *could* turn back to him and find power to live his life, *if they willed it*.

ONE

The Gracious Deeds of the Lord

Isaiah 63:7–9 *I will recount the gracious deeds of the* Lord, *the praiseworthy acts of the* Lord, *because of all that the* Lord *has done for us, and the great favor to the house of Israel that he has shown them according to his mercy, according to the abundance of his steadfast love.*

⁸For he said, "Surely they are my people, children who will not deal falsely"; and he became their savior ⁹in all their distress. It was no messenger or angel but his presence that saved them; in his love and in his pity he redeemed them; he lifted them up and carried them all the days of old.

Understanding the Word. Everything in our walk with God depends on him. That was true for Israel and it is true for us. Unless he had made the first move to come to us through his approach to Abraham some four thousand years ago, it is hard to imagine what condition the human race would be in today, if it existed at all.

Isaiah began by recalling all that God had *done* for his people. God has entered into time and space and has *acted* on our behalf. In the case of Israel, he took them to Egypt and brought them out again. He led them to the land he had promised and gave it to them. In spite of their failures in the Judges period, he made them into a great kingdom. When, in spite of all he had done for them, they persisted in their idolatry, he brought the great empires against them and took them into captivity. But after all that, he would not give up on them, and, against all the odds, restored them to their land. God is not merely some great mystical presence, a kind of benign cloud hovering over creation. He is at work in time and space in the lives of his people, and he gives us eyes to see that work if we will receive the gift.

But why is he so willing to work for us, and *persistently* willing to do so? The answer is found in the central emphasis of the passage. God works graciously for us because of his unique character. He is not like the gods, for they are simply human beings writ large. Thus, although they can be kind at times, they can never be trusted because, like the ordinary human, they are ruled by self-interest, and when that comes into play, everything else goes out the window. But Yahweh is not that way; he is consistently characterized by self-giving, self-denying love. This was such a remarkable concept in the ancient religious world, that it appears the Hebrews had to coin a word to convey it. It is the word *hesed*, unknown elsewhere among the Semitic languages, but occurring more than 250 times in the Hebrew Bible. In fact, this is actually how verse 7 begins: "I will mention the lovingkindnesses [*hasdim*, plural of *hesed*] of the LORD" (NKJV). His gracious actions in time and space are an expression of who he is. Being who he is, he could act in no other way. He is a God who relates to his creatures with compassion, mercy, love, and deep feeling (pity). We are not pawns on his chessboard, but his sheep, his children, his bride, his friends.

1. As you look back over your life, can you think of points where God acted on your behalf? If not, ask him to show you.

2. Many of us have negative images of God, at least in part because of childhood experiences with parents or others. If this is true for you, how might the understanding that God loves you unconditionally address those negative images?

3. What are the implications of the character of God for us and our lives?

TWO

But They Rebelled

Isaiah 63:10–14 *But they rebelled and grieved his holy spirit; therefore he became their enemy; he himself fought against them. ¹¹Then they remembered the days of old, of Moses his servant. Where is the one who brought them up out of the sea with the shepherds of his flock? Where is the one who put within them his holy spirit, ¹²who caused his glorious arm to march at the right hand of Moses, who divided the waters before them to make for himself an everlasting name, ¹³who led them through the depths? Like a horse in the desert, they did not stumble. ¹⁴Like cattle that go down into the valley, the spirit of the LORD gave them rest. Thus you led your people, to make for yourself a glorious name.*

Understanding the Word. This part of the chapter continues the earlier theme of remembrance. But now it focuses on God's response to what has been a continuing theme throughout the book of Isaiah: rebellion. This is not an accidental or unintentional sin, but one that has been committed in full knowledge that what we are doing is a violation of what our Father wishes and expects. Perhaps the author is thinking of the making of the golden calf, less than six weeks after their most solemn vow, sworn in blood, that they would never break their covenant with Yahweh. But in view of verse 11, "they remembered the days of old," it seems likely that the more recent rebellions are in view.

The prophet confessed on behalf of the people that they had grieved the Holy Spirit. This is a most remarkable statement, one that speaks of the very personal relationship that God is looking for with his people. We might expect a more formal word such as "offended," or even "insulted." But "grieved" suggests an intimate interpersonal relationship, where the action results in a feeling of hurt in the injured party (see 54:6 where it is said that an abandoned wife is "grieved in spirit"; see also Ephesians 4:30).

But that very thought that the relationship with God is more personal than legal calls to mind the origins of that relationship when God graciously led them out of Egypt, and put his Spirit into Moses and then the seventy elders (Num. 11:17, 25). They remembered how God led them, through the sea, and like cattle following a cowherd, they obediently followed him. The result of that event was that God gained an incredible reputation all over that region (see Joshua 2:10).

All this would have had great implications for the returnees. Surely, if God was this sort of God, one who was compassionate, slow to anger, and overflowing with lovingkindness (*hesed*), who would willingly forgive sin (Exod. 34:6–7), one who was not seeking his own self-interest, but longed for close, intimate relationships with his creatures; surely, he would forgive his people again and anew. All that is true, but the danger lies in the parallel suggestion that if such relationships don't exist, if we are sinful and unrepentant, then somehow that is God's problem. That is definitely not true.

1. Reflect on the concept of "grieving the Holy Spirit." What other implications does this have beyond the ones mentioned above? Look at Ephesians 4:30.

2. Why might someone think that if God desires relationships with us, and a breach has occurred, it is his responsibility to heal it in some way? Can you think of parallels in human affairs?

3. What is it in our human nature that makes us prone to rebellion, not only in respect to God, but in other relationships as well?

THREE

You Are Our Father

Isaiah 63:15–19 *Look down from heaven and see, from your holy and glorious habitation. Where are your zeal and your might? The yearning of your heart and your compassion? They are withheld from me.* ¹⁶*For you are our father, though Abraham does not know us and Israel does not acknowledge us; you, O LORD, are our father; our Redeemer from of old is your name.* ¹⁷*Why, O LORD, do you make us stray from your ways and harden our heart, so that we do not fear you? Turn back for the sake of your servants, for the sake of the tribes that are your heritage.* ¹⁸*Your holy people took possession for a little while; but now our adversaries have trampled down your sanctuary.* ¹⁹*We have long been like those whom you do not rule, like those not called by your name.*

Understanding the Word. Now the subtle implications in the previous statement come out into the open. What an amazing statement appears in verse 17, "Why, O LORD, do you make us stray from your ways and harden our heart?" God did not make them stray! This is like sheep who have wandered off in search of another tuft of grass, and find themselves lost, saying to the shepherd, "Why did you make us do that?"!

This vividly displays a second common characteristic of fallen humanity. The first is the one we have previously discussed: self-interest. The second is here: refusal to accept responsibility. Just as self-interest is evident in earliest childhood, so is denial of responsibility. The evidence is perfectly plain to see, but yet the child asserts with bland assurance, "I didn't do it." We learn early that to accept responsibility for unfortunate occurrences is to be liable for sometimes painful consequences, and so we deny responsibility. Also, if the occurrence was not our doing, then we have no responsibility to deal with the results, whether correcting them or counteracting them. That is what these people are doing. Their sanctuary has been destroyed, their land is now simply a tiny portion of the huge Persian Empire, and there is little evidence that their God is ruler of the universe. These are the consequences of their persistent refusal to obey the terms of the covenant they had entered into a thousand years earlier. But whose fault is it? It is their Father's fault! Who needs to repent ("turn back," v. 17)? Yahweh does! And why should he restore his people to prominence and power? Because they are "the tribes that are your heritage" (v. 17.) In other words, because God, not Abraham, had brought them into existence, and because he had declared that they were his special possession, his heritage, therefore, it was his responsibility to make them into the kind of people he wanted.

Such an attitude would be laughable if it were not so tragic. But it is also not humorous because we see it all around us. When people are chided for their outbursts of rage, they respond, "I can't help it, it's just the way I am." They may not bring God into the argument, but they are saying the same thing the ancient Judeans did. They refuse to admit that they have responsibility for the way they act, *and* that they have responsibility and the freedom to change that way of acting. But that would be to accept the burden of working on this character fault, and that is too hard. The result is that everyone around them suffers.

1. How are self-interest, denial of responsibility, and attempts to avoid expenditure of effort related?

2. Besides "That's just the way I am," what other excuses have you heard (or made!) in order to deny responsibility?

3. Why are the insistence upon personal freedom and the denial of responsibility incompatible?

FOUR

Oh, That You Would Tear Open the Heavens

Isaiah 64:1–5 *O that you would tear open the heavens and come down, so that the mountains would quake at your presence—²as when fire kindles brushwood and the fire causes water to boil—to make your name known to your adversaries, so that the nations might tremble at your presence! ³When you did awesome deeds that we did not expect, you came down, the mountains quaked at your presence. ⁴From ages past no one has heard, no ear has perceived, no eye has seen any God besides you, who works for those who wait for him. ⁵You meet those who gladly do right, those who remember you in your ways. But you were angry, and we sinned; because you hid yourself we transgressed.*

Understanding the Word. This part of chapter 64 continues the notes of the previous ones: remembering the demonstrations of both God's amazing power and his amazing grace extended to his people in the past, and the conclusion that since the people are not demonstrating his presence in the present, it must somehow be God's fault. This is a classic example of a faulty syllogism. A syllogism is a form of logical argument in which the truth of two premises establishes the truth of a conclusion: (1) living things all share certain characteristics; (2) a rock does not share these characteristics; (3) therefore, a rock is not a living thing. But if one or both of the premises are incorrect, then the conclusion will be incorrect. What are the premises here? (1) God has demonstrated his power and love to his people in the past; (2) the people are not now experiencing his power and love and are living in sin; (3) therefore,

God is hiding himself from them, *with the result that they are sinning.* What is wrong with that syllogism? The people have confused effect with cause. It is not because God is absent that they are sinning; it is because they are sinning that God is absent.

Even if the conclusion of the syllogism is false, the descriptions of God's character and actions are spot-on and will repay our reflection on them. Yahweh does indeed want to demonstrate his awesome power to the nations (vv. 2–3). But one of the primary ways he wants to demonstrate that power, now that Christ has made the Holy Spirit available to all of us through his death and resurrection, is in our lives. If we have been delivered from self-interest, and thereby enabled to live lives of outstanding faithfulness, integrity, and love, unlike so much of the rest of the human race, the delivering power of God will be unmistakable.

Furthermore, it is true that there is no God like the Yahweh who is revealed in the Bible. He alone is a transcendent God who is not of this world and, therefore, has unlimited power to accomplish his will. But, you might say, that is how the Muslim Allah is described. Yes, but we are not finished describing Yahweh. He *is* utterly transcendent (holy), but he is *also* self-giving, self-denying love. Nowhere else in all existence is there such a God. As Isaiah says in verse 4, no one has seen, or heard, or even thought of a God like this who is absolutely trustworthy. For that is the point of the phrase "works for those who wait for him." There is no limit to his power: he works. But neither is there any limit to his trustworthiness; we can wait in complete trust for him to act, knowing that his every inclination toward us is for our best.

1. Have you ever been guilty of a false syllogism like that the Judeans fell into? Why did you think that way?

2. Why is it so hard for us to wait for the Lord to act in our lives?

3. Where do you need to see God's power at work in your life today? What is your responsibility in order for that power to be unleashed?

FIVE

Will You Restrain Yourself?

Isaiah 64:6–12 *We have all become like one who is unclean, and all our righteous deeds are like a filthy cloth. We all fade like a leaf, and our iniquities, like the wind, take us away. ⁷There is no one who calls on your name, or attempts to take hold of you; for you have hidden your face from us, and have delivered us into the hand of our iniquity. ⁸Yet, O LORD, you are our Father; we are the clay, and you are our potter; we are all the work of your hand. ⁹Do not be exceedingly angry, O LORD, and do not remember iniquity forever. Now consider, we are all your people. ¹⁰Your holy cities have become a wilderness, Zion has become a wilderness, Jerusalem a desolation. ¹¹Our holy and beautiful house, where our ancestors praised you, has been burned by fire, and all our pleasant places have become ruins. ¹²After all this, will you restrain yourself, O LORD? Will you keep silent, and punish us so severely?*

Understanding the Word. It is perhaps too easy for us to pass judgment upon the Judeans, and to say that they should stop blaming God for their problems. But they had been brought face-to-face with the depths of the human problem. That problem is that we seem unable to defeat the power of sinning in our lives. We know we ought to do better in controlling our deep-seated passions for more pleasure, more possessions, more power, more approval, more of everything, and we make good resolutions to do better. Yet it seems the resolutions fail every time, and sometimes almost before we make them. Why are we so powerless in the face of our desires? As we have seen, the Judeans reasoned that since their experience had taught them that all power is in God's hands, then it must be his fault if they don't have the power to defeat sin in their lives. For some unknown reason, he was withholding that power from them.

We also have to give the Judeans credit for squarely facing their condition. There is no denying the reality of that condition, a practice that is all too easy for us humans. "Well," we say, "I'm no saint, but I'm surely not as bad as so-and-so. I have a few problems, but they're not too bad." Not so with these people. Their cities and their temple were in ruins, and those conditions were only too symbolic of the ruins in the character of the people who were living among those ruins. The repetition of "iniquities"/"iniquity" here (vv. 6, 7, 9), underlines the inescapable fact of their sin and its consequences. They had done those things and thought in those ways, and there was no escape from it.

Perhaps the most significant consequence of sin, as they recognized, is that it makes us unclean (v. 6) in the presence of the One who is absolutely clean. This powerful metaphor runs through the Bible. Clean and unclean are opposites; the one cannot exist in the presence of the other. If there are two surgeons operating on a patient, and one is thoroughly clean, while the other has not taken the time to scrub, the patient's wound *will* become contaminated. Long before anyone understood the necessity for sterility in the operating room, the biblical writers understood the contaminating power of sin. For the pagans, clean and unclean was a matter of exorcising evil powers so that rituals would be effective. Not so in the Bible. It is the damning power of self that makes it impossible for us creatures to coexist with God. This explains that profound statement in verse 6. How can doing what is right make us filthy? Very simply, it is when we do those right things for the wrong motives and purposes. We may give a large sum of money to our church. That is certainly the right thing to do. But why have we done it? Is it because we unselfishly love God and others? Or is it because selfishly we want to be known to ourselves (and probably to others) as very generous persons?

1. If you were completely candid about your relationship with God, how would you describe it? Why is this the case? What needs to happen to change it?

2. Reflect further on the statement that "our righteous deeds are like a filthy cloth" (v. 6). What other examples can you think of besides the one given above?

3. Why is it that we seem unable to solve the sin problem on our own?

COMMENTARY NOTES

i. Although I have commented on the word *hesed* ("gracious deeds," 63:7) in other books in this series, it is such an important concept that it merits repetition here. As I said above, the word only appears in Hebrew, and I suggest that this is because the concept is unique to the Hebrew Bible. The basic idea is of continuing action for another that is in no way deserved or earned by that other. It occurs more than 250 times in the Hebrew Bible, with about three quarters of the occurrences referring to God. I suggest that for a deity to behave in this way was so surprising in the context of the ancient world that the Hebrews had to coin a word to convey this remarkable idea. Some sense of how amazing it was to them is found in the repeated affirmation "Oh give thanks to the LORD, for he is good; and his steadfast love [*hesed*] endures forever" (e.g., Ps. 107:1).

The concept is so comprehensive in the ways in which it is used that there is no single English word that can convey all its dimensions. The same was true for Greek, which is somewhat surprising since Greek is known for its comprehensive vocabulary. Thus, the Greek translations of the Old Testament, known as the Septuagint, regularly translated *hesed* with a Greek word whose equivalent in English is "mercy." (This is the King James Version translation.) While "mercy" is not incorrect, it fails to connote either the persistence or the personal element involved in *hesed*. *Hesed* is not a casual one-time act, but an ongoing personal attachment. On the human level, it is the quality that Ruth demonstrated to her mother-in-law, Naomi.

For these reasons the modern translations of the Old Testament use a whole variety of words and phrases to try to capture some of the senses of the word. Besides "mercy," they include: love, grace, kindness, lovingkindness, steadfast love, loyal love, and several more. In the end, the concept is of that all-but-inexplicable self-giving, self-denying love that the members of the Trinity share with each other and with all creation. In the end, it is the only explanation for what Christ has done for us on the cross.

ii. In 63:9 the New Revised Standard Version reads, "in all their distress. It was no messenger or angel but his presence that saved them." This is in contrast to almost all the other English translations. They read something like, "In their affliction he was afflicted, and the angel of his presence saved them" (KJV). The meaning of the Hebrew is somewhat obscure and the NRSV is following the Septuagint. But the other ancient versions essentially follow the Hebrew.

The major issue is with one Hebrew word. A literal rendering would be something like, "In all their afflictions to him affliction." The problem is that the word interpreted "to him" is spelled like the similar-sounding "not." (Both are pronounced "lo.") The ancient Jewish commentators, called the Masoretes, were certainly not going to change the spelling of the text they had received, but they said that the word should still be understood as "to him." If we take the word as a negative, then the next word can hardly mean "affliction," and it must be respelled for some word meaning "ambassador" or "messenger" in parallel with the following "angel." All in all, the traditional English rendering seems to have the fewest problems.

iii. As mentioned previously, "rebellion" is a pervasive concept in Isaiah. Although the English terms are not that frequent (ten times in the New Revised Standard Version), the Hebrew terms in that semantic field occur more than thirty times. They appear five times in chapters 1 and 59, four times in chapter 53, twice in chapters 30, 43, and 50, and then once in chapters 3, 24, 31, 36, 44, 46, 48, 57, 58, 63, 65, and 66. Five different terms are used. The most frequent are forms of *pasha* (twenty times), which has a personal tone. It carries the idea of overstepping a boundary, and is often translated "to transgress." In 1:2, Yahweh says he has reared children, but they have rebelled. This is not a formal/legal relationship, but a familial one (so also 43:25, 27, and 48:8).

Marah (five times; 1:20; 30:9; 36:5; 50:5; 63:10) and *marad* (36:5) carry a more formal tone. This is the act of revolting against one's king or overlord. The rebel has been in an agreed-upon

formal relationship, and is now willfully repudiating it.

The fourth term *sarah* (1:5; 31:6; 59:13) connotes apostasy with the idea of overturning an accepted standard of behavior and belief, whereas the fifth, *sarar* (1:23; 30:1; 65:2) refers to a stubbornness that will not recognize any other way than its own.

Taken together, these terms speak of an intentional breaking of a relationship whose terms have been defined and, in most cases, at least tacitly accepted. But to remain in such a relationship would be to admit that someone else's wishes had priority over one's own. To the proud, self-centered human spirit, that is an unacceptable admission.

iv. In 63:10, 11, and 14 the NRSV renders "holy spirit" (vv. 10, 11) and "spirit" (v. 14) where many other translations have "Holy Spirit" and "Spirit." This small difference reflects a fairly significant theological judgment about the concept of the Holy Spirit in Old Testament times. Those whom the NRSV translation represents would argue that to capitalize the terms is to read back into the Old Testament a Trinitarian concept that only has its earliest roots in New Testament teachings. While we must be careful not to engage in thoughtless reading back, and must certainly allow for progress in dogma, there is reason to suspect that already in Old Testament times there was a sense that the spirit of God was thought to have a distinct personal identity, and was not merely another way of speaking about God.

There is not space here to go into a prolonged discussion, but two examples may be permitted. First, when David begs that God's Spirit not be taken from him, it seems that he is not merely talking about a sense of God's presence, but a genuine expression of God's empowering reality in his life. The second example is from this passage itself. The statement that the people had "grieved his Holy Spirit" (63:10 NIV) suggests a personal identity that is hard to ignore.

While we may certainly agree that no carefully articulated understanding of differing persons within the Godhead existed in the Old Testament, still the same distinctive ways of speaking about God that could only give rise to such an understanding in the era of the early church were already present in germinal form.

v. Imputed and imparted righteousness. One of the foundational theological principles of the Protestant Reformation was the idea that when a person repents of their sin and puts their faith in Jesus, that God imputes righteousness to him or her. That is, God cancels out the record of sin and considers the person to be righteous on the merits of Christ. As the first three chapters of Romans clearly teach, it is impossible for anyone to have a relationship with God on the basis of their own righteousness, so this imputed righteousness is necessary.

But is that the end of the matter? It is not, and to think so is to run the risk of falling into the error of believing that actual righteous living is neither necessary nor possible for the person in relationship with God through Christ. Clearly, God expects his people to live righteous lives. Yet it seems impossible for us to do this by our own strength. This is the point at which God imparts righteousness. That is, he enables us to live genuinely righteous lives by the power of the Holy Spirit. A full-orbed understanding of the Christian life must make room for both imputation and impartation.

WEEK FOUR

GATHERING DISCUSSION OUTLINE

A. Open session in prayer.

B. View video for this week's readings.

C. What general impressions and thoughts do you have after considering the video and reading the daily writings on these Scriptures?

D. Discuss questions selected from the daily readings.

    1. **KEY OBSERVATION:** Even if there are times when God's justice requires him to discipline us or punish us, his love for us remains; it is unconditional.

    DISCUSSION QUESTION: Many of us have negative images of God, at least in part because of childhood experiences with parents or others. If this is true for you, how might the understanding that God loves you unconditionally address those negative images?

    2. **KEY OBSERVATION:** Sometimes when a person is persistently rebellious they blame God for their condition, saying that he made them that way.

    DISCUSSION QUESTION: What is it in our human nature that makes us prone to rebellion, not only in respect to God, but in other relationships as well?

3. **KEY OBSERVATION:** It can be argued that denial of responsibility and refusal to expend effort to change both spring from the rule of self-interest in one's life.

   DISCUSSION QUESTION: How are self-interest, denial of responsibility, and attempts to avoid expenditure of effort related?

4. **KEY OBSERVATION:** If people are sinning, it is neither because God is absent, nor because he could not stop them.

   DISCUSSION QUESTION: Where do you need to see God's power at work in your life today? What is your responsibility in order for that power to be unleashed?

5. **KEY OBSERVATION:** We seem to be powerless to solve the sin problem on our own.

   DISCUSSION QUESTION: Why is it that we seem unable to solve the sin problem on our own?

E. What facts and information presented in the commentary portion of the lesson help you understand the weekly Scripture?

F. Close session with prayer.

Isaiah 59:15b–21; 63:1–6; 61:1–3

The Divine Warrior, the Anointed One, Comes

INTRODUCTION

The sections on either side of this one (56:9–59:15a and 63:7–66:17) have amply demonstrated the problem the Israelite people were facing: their inability to live righteous lives. In the sections previous to and following those (56:1–8 and 66:18–24), Yahweh had shown that he wanted righteous living, and that there was no barrier between him and anyone, including foreigners and eunuchs, who would live such lives. But the Israelites had been living flagrantly sinful lives, indulging in idolatrous attitudes, if not outright idolatrous practices, depending upon mechanically performed rituals, manifesting arrogance over their supposed righteousness, mistreating the poor, and blaming Yahweh for the problem that at least some of them, as represented by the prophet, recognized they had.

What should be done to correct this condition? Clearly, the very first thing was the kind of awareness of their condition that is exampled in 59:9–15a and 64:6–7. Second, was the true self-abasement and contrition spoken of in 57:15 and 66:2. Third, was the realization that in ourselves we humans are helpless to change our behavior (64:6–9). This is not the same thing as blaming God because we persistently sin (63:17; 64:5–6), but rather the realization that despite our best efforts, we cannot seem to stop sinning. Fourth, was a turning to God in the faith that if he would give them the spiritual power to live righteous lives, they would.

That undertaking on their, and our, behalf is expressed here in two parallel revelations of a Divine Warrior (57:15b–21; 63:1–6). If there is any question as to whether the two should be considered parallel, that ought to be laid to rest by the observation that both 59:16 and 63:5 make the same point although using different pronouns. In the last part of each verse the same statement occurs with only one word different ("wrath" versus "righteousness"). This Warrior comes to defeat his people's enemies and deliver them. But who are these enemies? No enemy nations are mentioned in 56:1–59:15a or in 63:7–66:24. The only oppression identified in those chapters is the oppression of persistent sin. If it is pointed out that the Warrior is victorious over Edom in 63:1–6, I would argue that this one occurrence of an enemy nation should not be used to override all the statements about sin as the enemy in the rest of the division. Rather, those statements ought to be used to interpret the use of Edom. As in chapter 33, Edom should be understood to represent everything in the world that opposes the kingdom of God. Thus, here Edom is sin embodied. The Warrior has come to do for his people what they cannot do for themselves: defeat the power of sin and enable them to live the righteous lives he calls for.

But who is this Warrior? 59:15b makes it clear that it is Yahweh himself, but then verse 16 adds an extra touch when it says that it is "his own arm . . . his righteousness" that accomplishes the deliverance. In chapters 49–53, his "arm" is his Servant, one of whose functions is to release "prisoners" (42:7). When we then see the same language applied to the announcement of the Messiah in 61:1, we can say that this Warrior is the Messiah himself, come to defeat sin in a climactic way.

ONE

His Own Arm Brought Him Victory

Isaiah 59:15b–17 *The* Lord *saw it, and it displeased him that there was no justice.* [16]*He saw that there was no one, and was appalled that there was no one to intervene; so his own arm brought him victory, and his righteousness upheld him.* [17]*He put on righteousness like a breastplate, and a helmet of salvation on his head; he put on garments of vengeance for clothing, and wrapped himself in fury as in a mantle.*

Understanding the Word. As I mentioned in the introduction, there are clues here that this Warrior is identical to the Servant of chapters 40–55. One of these appears in verse 15b: "there was no justice." As I stated in the commentary in Week Three, the term "justice" refers to God's governmental order of the world. When sin rules in human affairs, God's justice is not to be found (as, for example, in 59:14). Sinful living necessarily violates God's order for life, with very predictable results in society. The Servant/Messiah comes to address that problem (see also 42:3–4). In the first place, he comes as a sacrificial lamb (53:7) to deliver us humans from the death sentence that sin has brought upon us. He delivers us from the curse of sin that requires we be separated from our Creator forever by taking upon himself the just sentence for our sin. But what about our inability to stop sinning? In the words of the apostle Paul, "Should we continue in sin in order that grace may abound?" (Rom. 6:1). Do we live out the rest of our lives going on doing the things that killed Christ in the first place? Paul's answer to the question is: "By no means!" (Rom. 6:2). To do that would mean a continued lack of justice in the world.

How are we to address the problem? We cannot do it on our own, as Isaiah 59:16 tells us. There is no one, humanly speaking, who can intervene and solve the problem. So the Warrior does it for us. Notice that now he is no longer the sacrificial lamb. Now he does not come to die for us, but to fight for us. He can do so because of his own righteousness. As the New Testament consistently tells us, Jesus Christ was without sin (2 Cor. 5:21; Heb. 4:15; 7:26; 1 Pet. 2:22; 1 John 3:5). This means that he can defeat sin for us, and on our behalf. His righteousness is his "breastplate" and his "helmet" is salvation. The apostle Paul used these same figures in his admonition to Christians to put on "the whole armor of God" (Eph. 6:13–17), so he clearly has this passage in mind. Because Christ has put on this armor for us, we, too, can put it on. His righteousness and his deliverance can be ours, and as he won the victory for us, we, too, can live in victory.

But what is the significance of "vengeance" and "fury" in Isaiah 59:17? What is he angry at? He is furious over what the enemy sin is doing to his creatures. He made us to live in harmony with him and with one another. But sin has entered the picture and is destroying God's creatures. God hates that, and we should as well. Sin is not something to be coddled and excused. It is not a little mistake or a little slip-up. It is an offense against the very fabric of creation, and ought to be eradicated everywhere we find it, especially in ourselves.

1. Why does our persistent sinning require the Messiah to come as a Warrior?

2. Why is it that we cannot defeat sin on our own?

3. What is the root cause of our continuing sin?

T W O

Wrath to His Adversaries; Redeemer to Those in Jacob

Isaiah 59:18–21 *According to their deeds, so will he repay; wrath to his adversaries, requital to his enemies; to the coastlands he will render requital.* *[19]So those in the west shall fear the name of the LORD, and those in the east, his glory; for he will come like a pent-up stream that the wind of the LORD drives on.*

[20]And he will come to Zion as Redeemer, to those in Jacob who turn from transgression, says the LORD.

[21]And as for me, this is my covenant with them, says the LORD: my spirit that is upon you, and my words that I have put in your mouth, shall not depart out of your mouth, or out of the mouths of your children, or out of the mouths of your children's children, says the LORD, from now on and forever. deny self + follow him

Understanding the Word. Here we see the two sides of the Warrior's work. On the one hand, he comes to work vengeance on his enemies; namely, the persistent sin in his people's lives (v. 18). His enmity against it is that if left unaddressed, it would make the people themselves his enemies (see 1:24–25), something that grieves him deeply. So, on the other hand, he comes to deliver his people from that enemy (v. 20).

One of the important notes here is the extent of his victory. "Coastlands" (v. 18) is a figure for the ends of the earth, and when this is coupled with "west" to "east," it signifies the whole earth. Sin has no chance against the mighty power of God, thus, as 66:18–19 tells us, there will come a day when the whole earth will recognize the truth of what Isaiah came to know in his temple vision: "the whole earth is full of his glory" (6:3). That is, it is God's significance and reality that makes the earth what it is, not the "fading flower" of humanity (see 28:1, 4). In the end, God's victory over sin in all its forms—personal, institutional, and otherwise—will be unmistakable, and those who seek to deny it will be swept away (see Revelation 6:15–16).

Having wrought vengeance on his enemy, sin, God will redeem his people "Jacob" (v. 20). But notice that there is a condition. That condition is that they turn from their "transgression" (not merely their sin). The specificity here is important. As I noted in the commentary on Week Four, the concept behind transgression is that of willfully violating someone's directions or wishes, thus, of rebellion. If Yahweh is to deliver us from our persistent sinning, we will have to willingly give up our insistence on having our own way at all costs. While we cannot stop sinning merely by willing to do so, neither can the Divine Warrior deliver us from sinning without our making that full surrender of our own will and way.

Verse 21 is tantalizing in its obscurity. On the surface, it seems to be addressed to "you," the prophet, and to be making a promise to him for the sake of the people ("them"). But the promise is very strange. It is one thing to give the Spirit to a prophet to enable him to speak a divine word to his people. But to "your children" and "your children's children . . . forever"? Nowhere else in the Bible is there a suggestion that prophecy was a family business lasting forever. (On "sons of the prophets," see the commentary notes at the end of the week.) Furthermore, the mention of the Spirit in connection with the defeat of persistent sinning is very much in line with New Testament teaching about the Spirit (see especially Romans 8). In that light, it is at least possible that "them" is the world, and that "you" is the people of God. That would mean that this is a promise of the coming of the Holy Spirit like those in chapters 36 and 44 (see also Ezekiel 36:27 and Joel 2:28), enabling the Jewish people who responded to the gospel (which includes the promise of Pentecost) to fulfill the mission to the world that Isaiah had promised (see 2:1–5). This also provides a transition into the vision of righteous Israel being a lamp through which God's light can shine on the nations in the very next verses (60:1–3).

1. What does it mean to see God's glory?

2. How does turning away from transgression relate to the surrender of our will to God?

3. Why is such a surrender necessary in order for God to deliver us from persistent sinning?

THREE

Who Is This?

Isaiah 63:1–3 *"Who is this that comes from Edom, from Bozrah in garments stained crimson? Who is this so splendidly robed, marching in his great might?"*

"It is I, announcing vindication, mighty to save."

[2]"Why are your robes red, and your garments like theirs who tread the wine press?"

[3]"I have trodden the wine press alone, and from the peoples no one was with me; I trod them in my anger and trampled them in my wrath; their juice spattered on my garments, and stained all my robes."

Understanding the Word. As I mentioned in the introduction, Edom here is symbolic of the world in rebellion against God. Bozrah was Edom's capital city. (For more on Edom, see the commentary notes at the end of the week.) Once again, the image is of a "splendidly robed" Warrior, who here is returning from battle victorious. His garments are stained red with the blood of his fallen enemies. For most of Israel's history, juice was extracted from grapes by putting the grapes in a vat hewn from stone and having several people stamp up and down on the grapes with their bare feet. The juice would run out of a small hole drilled at the bottom of the vat. Inevitably, any of the clothing worn by the people doing the stamping would be stained with juice spurting out of the grapes, and that is the source of the imagery here.

For those of us who have been blessed to see little or no warfare, this language seems excessively graphic, but for people of the ancient world over whom war may have swept several times in a lifetime, it was probably rather commonplace. The point is to talk about the total victory of the Warrior over his enemies. In the context of chapters 56–66, these enemies whom the Warrior has completely destroyed are the sins which his people have proven unable to

Wesleyan
Prevenient Grace -
God pulling us
Gen 3:15
Justification
Grace
Sanctifying Grace

Week Five

defeat. Thus, while we recoil from the language, the import of the language is good news: we do not have to live in the bondage of sin. The Warrior has defeated it conclusively, and we can live lives of integrity, moderation, generosity, and self-giving love, with our passions under the firm control of a will that is surrendered to our Maker. That is good news indeed!

I want to say one further thing about those bloody garments. Whose blood is it that stains the Messiah's garments? Is it the blood of his enemies? Yes. But who are the enemies? The blood is his own! As the Scriptures tell us, "For our sake he made him to be sin who knew no sin, so that in him we might become the righteousness of God" (2 Cor. 5:21). Jesus Christ became the enemy, and when he defeated the enemy, it was his own blood that stained his garments. He took our sin upon himself and conquered it forever, so that the guilt of our sin being forgiven, and the power of sin having been broken in us, we could live righteous lives, no glory to us but all glory to God.

The response in verse 1 is literally, "It is I, speaking in righteousness, mighty to save." (For a discussion of why the New Revised Standard Version translates the second clause as "announcing vindication," see the commentary on righteousness in Week Three.) Here it seems to me that this translation is even less justified than elsewhere. I believe the point is that the Warrior is speaking out of his own righteousness (see 59:16–17). That is, his righteousness has made him eminently able to defeat sin in a thorough way and, thus, to offer his people a complete salvation.

1. Why is "sinning religion" (i.e., the idea that if you say the right things and believe the right things, it does not matter how you actually live) an offense to the gospel?

2. What do you need to do in your own life to receive all the benefits of Christ's death?

3. What are some of the excuses that Christian people offer for their sinful behavior?

FOUR

A Day of Vengeance, a Year for My Redeeming

Isaiah 63:4–6 *"For the day of vengeance was in my heart, and the year for my redeeming work had come. ⁵I looked, but there was no helper; I stared, but there was no one to sustain me; so my own arm brought me victory, and my wrath sustained me. ⁶I trampled down peoples in my anger, I crushed them in my wrath, and I poured out their lifeblood on the earth."*

Understanding the Word. In this passage, we see reminiscences of 59:15b–21, as well as a repetition of the language of verses 1–3. There are two important points that should be made. The first one has to do with verse 4 and its relationship to 61:2 that we will discuss tomorrow. Hebrew poetry is characterized by the repetition of one key point in two or more synonymous statements. The two may seem different, but they are making the same point. (For more on Hebrew poetry, see the commentary notes at the end of the week.) Verse 4 is not saying two contrasting things, but one thing (as is 61:2). It is saying that for the Warrior to complete his work of redemption, he must take vengeance on all the sin that is preventing his people from experiencing the full meaning of their redemption. In short, there is no redemption apart from vengeance. We tend to think of vengeance as taking revenge on people who have offended us, but that is not the point here. God is attacking all that is destroying his people; namely, sin and its power.

The second important point in this passage is made in verse 5, which is, with only a few words' difference, a repetition of 59:16, but in the first person. Why repeat the point that there was no one else to redeem? Both in Jeremiah (30:13, 17) and Ezekiel (22:30; 34:6) a similar point is made. The repetition is to undergird the fact that no human in himself or herself has the capacity to defeat sin, let alone in the whole human race. If sin is ever to be defeated, and the race redeemed, it will be God alone who does it. The idea that I can make myself good enough for God by myself is sheer folly and, indeed, is the essence of sin. For to have such an attitude is to say that I do not need God, that I am self-sufficient, and that is exactly what all sin is about, and the fount from which all sins spring.

There are two slight differences between 59:16 and 63:5. First, in 59:16 the Warrior is appalled that there is no one else but he to intervene on behalf of his people, whereas in 63:5 he finds that there is no one to help him in the task. (We may think of the sleeping disciples in the garden of Gethsemane.) In either case, the point is the same: he alone must perform the task. The second difference in the two statements is that in 59:16, the Warrior's righteousness sustains him, whereas in 63:5, it is his wrath. These are two sides of the same concept. It is because of God's unfailing rightness that the wrong that now pervades the earth makes him so angry. His anger is not merely an emotional response to earth's rebellion ("How dare they do that to me!"), but it is because of what we are doing to ourselves that is such a defilement of all that he ever envisioned for us.

1. Are there times that you feel powerless against sin in your life? In the light of 59:15b–21 and 63:1–6, what do you need to do?

2. What specific sins in your life does the Warrior need to take vengeance upon?

3. What is your response when you think of the blood that stains the Warrior's garments?

FIVE

The LORD Has Anointed Me

Isaiah 61:1–3 *The spirit of the Lord GOD is upon me, because the LORD has anointed me; he has sent me to bring good news to the oppressed, to bind up the brokenhearted, to proclaim liberty to the captives, and release to the prisoners; ²to proclaim the year of the LORD's favor, and the day of vengeance of our God; to comfort all who mourn; ³to provide for those who mourn in Zion—to give them a garland instead of ashes, the oil of gladness instead of mourning, the mantle of praise instead of a faint spirit. They will be called oaks of righteousness, the planting of the LORD, to display his glory.*

Understanding the Word. Here we come to the center point and the climax of the division comprised of chapters 56–66. It is because of the work of the

Anointed One, the Messiah, that it will be possible for the people of God to be victorious over sin and to become a clean lamp through which the light of God may shine out in salvation for the whole world. If there were any question that this is the import of this passage, it should be laid to rest by Jesus using it, as reported in Luke 4, to announce his messiahship. It also serves to show that the Warrior of chapters 59 and 63 is none other than the Suffering Servant of chapters 42, 49–50, and 52–53 as it combines elements from both those representations of his ministry (42:7 = 61:1b; 61:2 = 63:4).

As noted on Day Four, it is important to underline the second of the two combinations. In Luke 4:18–19, where Christ's reading from the Isaiah scroll is quoted, some commentators note that the quotation stops with "the year of the Lord's favor" and say that Jesus did this intentionally to say that there is no vengeance in the Christian gospel. That is a fallacious interpretation. There can be little doubt that Jesus read the entire sentence, which extends through verse 3. But for purposes of the text of Luke, it was sufficient to quote just the first part of the sentence. There is no question that Jesus' understanding of redemption included the necessity to destroy sin in all its power (Mark 9:42–48; John 8:34–36; Romans 6:10; 1 John 3:8).

Clearly the work of the Messiah, as described here, is to deliver from oppression, bondage, sorrow, and despair ("faint spirit"). In the context of this division of the book, all of those are a result of sin. Persons laboring under the bondage and oppression of sin will be subject to grief and despair. But Jesus has come to deliver us from that bondage. Of course, the Christian will have occasion to be sorrowful and oppressed; this is a fallen world after all. But we need not be in bondage to persistent sinning, with no witness to the world that is looking on. Rather we can be "oaks of righteousness, the planting of the LORD, to display his glory" (v. 3). This is the birthright of the servants of Yahweh. This is what Jesus died for, not merely that we can be freed from guilt and go to heaven, but that we might share the righteousness of God, and be lights in a dark and darkening world. (On the relationship of the Messiah to the Spirit (v. 1), see the commentary notes at the end of the week.)

1. Why is it appropriate to speak of the impact of sin in our lives as one of bondage and oppression?

2. How does Jesus' statement, "Blessed are those who mourn" (Matt. 5:4), relate to this passage?

3. If someone were to say to you, "It just seems like I can't stop doing that, even though I know it's wrong," what would you say to them in the light of our study thus far?

COMMENTARY NOTES

i. Those who are familiar with the King James Version will be somewhat surprised at the way modern versions translate 59:19b. The KJV reads: "When the enemy shall come in like a flood, the Spirit of the LORD shall lift up a standard against him," whereas all modern translations agree closely with the NRSV rendering: "for he will come like a pent-up stream that the wind of the LORD drives on."

The two translations, seemingly very different, are the result of four issues in the Hebrew. First, while the opening preposition could be rendered "when," it occurs much more frequently as a causal particle, thus "for" or "because" is more probable. Second, the subject of the third person verb "come" is not identified. It is simply "he." "Enemy" is provided by the KJV translators, and is not very likely. Third, the KJV translators did not understand correctly the verb form *nossah* (which only occurs here). They thought it was related to the noun *nes*, "banner," so they speculated that the verb meant "to raise a banner." However, further study has shown that the root is *nus*, meaning "to flee," and this form of the verb thus means "to drive." Finally, in the light of the rest of the rendering, it seems best to translate the word that can mean either "wind" or "spirit" with "wind."

ii. In relation to the statement in Day Two that there is no indication that prophecy was a family business, we need to discuss the phrase "the sons of the prophets" (2 Kings 2:3ff KJV). Hebrew uses the term often translated "son" (*ben*) in a variety of ways. While it can refer to a physical descendant (thus, "son," "grandson," "descendant"), it also is used to refer to members of a class. So when Nebuchadnezzar saw a fourth figure in the furnace and said it looked like "a son of the gods" (Dan. 3:25 NIV), he meant that it looked like a member of the class of beings known as gods. Thus, the phrase "sons of the prophets" almost certainly does not mean "the male children of the prophets," but a "group of people of the prophet class." Thus, NIV and NRSV have "the company of the prophets," while NLT has "the group of prophets."

iii. The region of Edom was south and east of Judah. While its home territory was in the rift south of the Dead Sea and in the mountains to the east of the rift (Bosrah was located in those mountains), the Edomites were constantly pushing westward toward the more fertile areas in the southern part of Judah. This occasioned continual hostility between Judah and Edom. However, there were confrontations over territory with other nations, notably the Philistines, that did not evoke the same level of hostility as with Edom. The Bible roots the origins of the hostility in the sibling rivalry between the ancestors of the two nations: Jacob and Esau. But it went beyond that. In Obadiah, we see an Edom that saw in the Babylonian conquest an opportunity to displace

Judah completely. It was not merely a matter of territory, but an antipathy to the very existence of the Israelites. It appears that it is that kind of attitude that explains the use of Edom as the image of the world. It does not merely contend with the people of God for dominance; it wishes to destroy them completely. It is not a matter of coexistence, but of destruction.

iv. As mentioned previously, Hebrew poetry is characterized by the phenomenon that has come to be known as "parallelism," that is, the making of a single point by means of two or more usually synonymous statements. I say "usually" because it is also possible to make the point using opposing statements. There are many examples of this form in the book of Proverbs. Here is one example: "The sacrifice of the wicked is an abomination to the LORD, but the prayer of the upright is his delight" (Prov. 15:8). While there were normally three accent units in each of the two parts, it is clear that the Hebrew poets were not slaves to form and enjoyed introducing variations. In recent years, it has become clear that there were some fixed pairs, that is, if the poet used a certain word in the first line, it was expected that he use the standard equivalent in the second. "Heaven" and "earth" are such a pair. But again, there was no slavish adherence to such expectations. The important thing in interpreting this poetry is not to play the pair against each other, but to use them together, allowing each to illuminate the other.

v. Anointing refers to the pouring of sacred oil upon a person's head as a way of representing their being consecrated and set apart for special service. The practice was not unique to Israel, but the Old Testament reports it in greater detail than is found elsewhere. The verb usually translated "anoint" (*mashach*) only means "to put oil upon," so context is very important in understanding what is taking place in various references. There were special instructions for preparing the sacred oil, and it was forbidden to make and apply this oil for non-sacred purposes (Exod. 30:23ff.). This was almost certainly because anointing was a symbol of Yahweh's appointment and consecration for office.

In the Old Testament, it was primarily prophets (1 Kings 19:16), priests (Exod. 28:41), and kings (1 Sam. 10:1) who were anointed, with kings being referred to most often. Both prophets and priests were involved in the royal anointing. A person upon whom the oil was poured was understood to be empowered by the Spirit for service. Thus, a person chosen by God for special service could be referred to as "the anointed" (*meshiach*, "messiah") whether or not they had actually had the oil poured on them (e.g., the Persian emperor Cyrus is said to be Yahweh's "anointed" in Isaiah 45:1). When the speaker in 61:1 says he has been anointed by Yahweh himself with the result that the Spirit is upon him, it is a signal statement of that person's divine appointment and empowerment.

vi. In the book of Isaiah, there is a special connection between the Holy Spirit and the Messiah. It is seen first in chapter 11, where it is said that the Spirit of the Lord will rest on him and that the Spirit will give him unusual wisdom, understanding, and knowledge (11:2). Again, in 42:1, Yahweh says that he had put his Spirit upon the Servant who will bring God's justice into the world. Finally, it is stated again in 61:1. These occurrences help to explain what took place at Jesus' baptism, as reported in Matthew, Mark, and Luke. John was troubled by Jesus' request to be baptized, but Jesus said it was necessary to do the right thing ("to fulfill all righteousness," Matt. 3:15). When he was baptized, the Spirit came upon him. Almost certainly, this was Jesus' anointing ceremony. The priesthood in Jerusalem was corrupt; they could not anoint him, even if they would. And while Jesus, as second person of the Trinity, hardly needed the baptism of the Spirit, it was important to show that he truly was the Anointed One, on whom the Spirit rested, in fulfillment of all the Old Testament promises.

WEEK FIVE

GATHERING DISCUSSION OUTLINE

A. Open session in prayer.

B. View video for this week's readings.

C. What general impressions and thoughts do you have after considering the video and reading the daily writings on these Scriptures?

D. Discuss questions selected from the daily readings.

> **1.** **KEY OBSERVATION:** Despite our best efforts, we humans seem to be unable to defeat our persistent sinning.
>
> **DISCUSSION QUESTION:** Why is it that we cannot defeat sin on our own?

> **2.** **KEY OBSERVATION:** One of the key elements in finding victory over persistent sinning is the surrender of our will.
>
> **DISCUSSION QUESTION:** How does turning away from transgression relate to the surrender of our will to God?

> **3.** **KEY OBSERVATION:** Many Christians believe that it is impossible to live a life of victory over sin. Yet the apostle Paul tells us the Christians must not continue to sin.
>
> **DISCUSSION QUESTION:** Why is "sinning religion" (i.e., the idea that if you say the right things and believe the right things, it does not matter how you actually live) an offense to the gospel?

4. **KEY OBSERVATION:** God is furious that there are sins which keep defeating his people and in Christ he has taken vengeance upon them and defeated them.

   DISCUSSION QUESTION: What specific sins in your life does the Warrior need to take vengeance upon?

5. **KEY OBSERVATION:** In the overall context of the passages studied this week, it is clear that here Isaiah describes the impact of sin in our lives as one of bondage and oppression.

   DISCUSSION QUESTION: Why is it appropriate to speak of the impact of sin in our lives as one of bondage and oppression?

E. What facts and information presented in the commentary portion of the lesson help you understand the weekly Scripture?

F. Close session with prayer.

Isaiah 60

Arise, Shine, for Your Light Has Come

INTRODUCTION

With the work of the Anointed One, the Divine Warrior, accomplished, Israel is now in a position to realize the larger purpose of her servanthood—namely, a witness to the nations. The imagery is of a lamp whose wick had been untrimmed. The flame was guttering and smoky, fitful at best. That was sinful Israel, in whom the light of God was obscured. But now that the Warrior has reproduced his own character in his people, the character of righteousness and justice, the wick is trimmed, and the light of God goes forth undimmed. It is the light of God that has dawned, of course. It is not Israel's own light that can illuminate a dark world. We, the people of God, can only be the lamp; the flame is God's. But we *are* the lamp. What an amazing thing! God chooses to use us, his people, to be the light-bearers. Unless we are allowing him to do all he wants to in us, the world will never know the good news. They will see so-called Christians whose lives are no different from those around them, people who act as though material satisfaction is all that is worth living for, people who are grasping and unforgiving, people whose word is worthless, people who are on the take, people who are dominated by self-interest, and they will never see the blazing glory of God. But if we *do* manifest the supernatural character of God, they will see him and be drawn to him.

A dominant theme of this chapter is one that it picks up from chapter 2: the coming of the nations to Jerusalem. Because of the light that shines forth, all the nations come (v. 2). Although it is not made explicit here, they clearly come because, as 2:3 says, "he [will] teach us his ways." They have seen those ways exampled in the lives of the New Israel, and are drawn to the God of

Israel. This is what happened in the first centuries after Christ: people who were disillusioned with the tired paganism of the Roman Empire saw something in the lives of Christians that gave them hope for new life.

Here, the coming of the nations to Jerusalem has two by-products: they will bring Israel's scattered children home, and they will bring their wealth to adorn the temple, the place of God's glory (see especially v. 9). Furthermore, those who once oppressed Israel will now serve Israel and all violence against God's people will cease forever (vv. 14, 18). These ideas flow naturally into an eschatological vision of that day when Yahweh will be all in all for his people and they will display his splendor in righteousness forevermore (vv. 19–22).

final destination
of soul and human kind

ONE

Nations Will Come to Your Light

Isaiah 60:1–3 *Arise, shine; for your light has come, and the glory of the LORD has risen upon you. ²For darkness shall cover the earth, and thick darkness the peoples; but the LORD will arise upon you, and his glory will appear over you. ³Nations shall come to your light, and kings to the brightness of your dawn.*

Understanding the Word. These few verses express the biblical perspective on life and the world. The world is in darkness, unable to produce light. This is so because God alone is the source of light. But God has chosen to put his light in human beings for the sake of other human beings. Just as a fire at night seems to exercise an almost hypnotic effect upon people, so the light of God shining out of human lives is powerfully attractive. When they come to see the light, they become the next generation of light-bearers.

What is the darkness that characterizes the world? There is no better description than that found in Paul's letter to the Galatians: "Now the works of the flesh are obvious: fornication, impurity, licentiousness, idolatry, sorcery, enmities, strife, jealousy, anger, quarrels, dissensions, factions, envy, drunkenness, carousing, and things like these" (Gal. 5:19–21a). It is interesting that the list begins and ends with the more physical aspects of the darkness: sexual immorality and drunken carousing, while the more attitudinal aspects are in the middle. It is not possible to say whether this ordering was intentional for the apostle, but we may say that while the darkness may manifest itself in the more obviously gross behaviors, its deeper manifestation is in the attitudes that result in social disorder. However these features are organized, they all stem from one overriding human desire: the need to satisfy my needs for myself in my way. This is "the heart of darkness," to borrow a book title from Joseph Conrad.

The theme of "glory" (vv. 1–2) recurs throughout the book of Isaiah (from 2:10 to 66:19) more than forty times. We have had occasion to speak elsewhere about the somewhat unusual, to our way of thinking, connotation of the Hebrew word. It is not merely a passing gleam, but weightiness, or significance. A person who has made something of himself or herself has glory. But the question is: Where is the source of true glory? Chapter 6 says it all: the earth is full of Yahweh's glory. Thus, any supposed glory achieved apart from him and his purposes truly is evanescent, a passing fancy. It is when we surrender our thirst for our own glory, and find it in him, that we become truly people of worth and significance. This is one aspect of what Christ came to do (see John 17:1–5, 22); when God is glorified in our lives by means of Christ living in us, the purposes of the cross, the resurrection, and Pentecost are achieved.

1. What is the evidence of God's glory in people whom the world might call insignificant?

2. What does it mean to "walk in the light, as he himself is in the light" (1 John 1:7)?

3. What is it about God's light that attracts people to it? Is that light shining in you?

TWO

Lift up Your Eyes

Isaiah 60:4–9 *Lift up your eyes and look around; they all gather together, they come to you; your sons shall come from far away, and your daughters shall be carried on their nurses' arms. ⁵Then you shall see and be radiant; your heart shall thrill and rejoice, because the abundance of the sea shall be brought to you, the wealth of the nations shall come to you. ⁶A multitude of camels shall cover you, the young camels of Midian and Ephah; all those from Sheba shall come. They* *shall bring gold and frankincense, and shall proclaim the praise of the LORD. ⁷All the flocks of Kedar shall be gathered to you, the rams of Nebaioth shall minister to you; they shall be acceptable on my altar, and I will glorify my glorious house. ⁸Who are these that fly like a cloud, and like doves to their windows? ⁹For the coastlands shall wait for me, the ships of Tarshish first, to bring your children from far away, their silver and gold with them, for the name of the LORD your God, and for the Holy One of Israel, because he has glorified you.*

Understanding the Word. One of the great fears of the Israelite people when they went into exile was that they would disappear as a people. Their children would become Babylonians and the people of God would cease to exist as a people (43:5). But Isaiah had said that it would not happen; God would keep his promise to Abraham, and his descendants would not cease to exist (44:1–5; 49:22–23). Here, that promise is renewed. The former oppressors themselves would bring Jerusalem's children back to her (vv. 4, 9). That promise has been fulfilled again and again through the ages, most recently in the forming of the state of Israel. Logically, the Jewish people should have disappeared centuries ago, given all the forces ranged against them, but it has not happened. God keeps his promises.

Not only will the former oppressors bring back Israel's children, they will also bring their wealth. Israel had been destroyed, all the wealth that had been acquired through the years carried off. Now God promises that all that wealth would be restored. The imagery used here underscores the worldwide origins of this wealth. It would come from southern Arabia ("Sheba") in Midianite camel caravans coming up from the port of Elath on the Red Sea (v. 6). It would also come from the more immediate east beyond the Dead Sea in the form of flocks and herds. (On Kedar and Nebaioth, see the commentary notes at the end of the week.) Then from the surging west would come "ships of Tarshish" (v. 9) with silver and gold. Tarshish almost certainly referred to the far western end of the Mediterranean Sea, which was thought to be at the ends of the earth (expressed as "coastlands"). Ships of Tarshish referred to any of the great merchant ships plying the Mediterranean.

The purpose of all this wealth was not merely the enrichment of the people of Judah and Jerusalem. Rather, it was for the glorifying of God (v. 7) and for the honor of his name (v. 9). Yahweh's name had been profaned by the people having to go into exile, so by restoring them (against all odds) and having his temple rebuilt, his name would be hallowed once again (Ezek. 35:20ff).

The statement that "the coastlands shall wait for me" (v. 9) echoes the same thought found in 51:5 where it says, "the coastlands wait for me, and for my arm they hope." "Wait" in the Old Testament is synonymous with "trust in." So these two statements are a way of saying that there would come a day when people of every race and family from all over the world would trust God for salvation from sin and despair. "Arm" in chapters 50–53 is a reference to God's power to deliver, a power that was displayed in a most unlikely form in the Servant (52:13–53:12), who gave himself up for the transgressions (rebellions) of his people. That same "Arm" would be for all the world.

1. What does the fulfillment of God's promises for the children of Abraham mean for the fulfillment of his promises for his church?

2. How can we profane God's name, and on the other hand, how can we hallow it (see Matthew 6:9)?

3. Why are waiting and trusting synonymous?

THREE
Foreigners Will Build up Your Walls

Isaiah 60:10–14 *Foreigners shall build up your walls, and their kings shall minister to you; for in my wrath I struck you down, but in my favor I have had mercy on you. *[11]*Your gates shall always be open; day and night they shall not be shut, so that nations shall bring you their wealth, with their kings led in procession. *[12]*For the nation and kingdom that will not serve you shall perish; those nations shall be utterly laid waste. *[13]*The glory of Lebanon shall come to you, the cypress, the plane, and the pine, to beautify the place of my sanctuary; and I will glorify where my feet rest. *[14]*The descendants of those who oppressed you shall come bending low to you, and all who despised you shall bow down at your feet; they shall call you the City of the LORD, the Zion of the Holy One of Israel.*

Understanding the Word. On the surface, what is said in this segment seems to contradict what I said in the previous segment; namely, that the nations would come to Jerusalem trusting in the God who revealed himself there. Here we see foreign kings being "led in procession" (v. 11) as slaves to Jerusalem, where they bow in submission (v. 14). They will serve Israel by rebuilding the walls they once tore down (v. 10) and if they won't submit they will perish (v. 12). How can we reconcile these two apparently contradictory affirmations? Are the foreign nations coming as slaves or as fellow believers?

The answer to the question is yes. There can be no question that in the book as a whole the foreigners are intended by God to become his worshippers and followers (2:1–5; 49:6; 56:1–8; 66:18–23). So, what was said in 60:9 is correct. But, the other affirmation is correct as well. The nations have a choice as to how they bow in submission before Yahweh. They can do it willingly and joyfully, or they can do it involuntarily and resentfully. So it is said in Philippians 2:10 that every knee shall bow before Jesus. That is, the fact of his lordship will be unmistakable—no one will be able to deny it—but some will bow involuntarily. That is the side of the coin being addressed in these verses. The kings of the earth will either work *with* redeemed Israel or work *for* her. We don't need to ask when this was or will be literally fulfilled. The point is that Israel need not fear the nations of the earth if she will but trust Yahweh. Those nations are the ones that must come to terms with Israel's God in one way or another.

Once again we see the theme of glory (v. 13). Just as long before in the reign of Solomon, the lumber from Lebanon had been used to beautify the wonderful temple that Solomon built, so again those resources and others will be used to manifest God's glory. To ask which temple is being talked about here, whether the second (516 BC), Herod's, or some future one, is the wrong question. God is making the point that all of earth's resources must in the end glorify him. Exactly how that will happen is up to him, and we do not need to know.

Notice that "the Holy One of Israel" appears twice in this chapter (vv. 9 and 14). This epithet that is so common in the book (twenty-five times, twenty-six if we count "Holy One of Jacob" in 29:23) speaks of both Yahweh's transcendence (he is the only one in the universe truly qualified to be called holy—other) and his immanence (in his transcendence he has yet bound himself to a small and insignificant people—Israel). For the nations to recognize him in this way is to recognize him in his true uniqueness. There is none like him.

1. If, in the end, persons will no longer be able to deny that Jesus is Lord, why might they still refuse to give him their hearts?

2. What does this say about the true nature of sin?

3. Practically speaking, what should it mean in our lives if we call Yahweh "the Holy One of Israel"?

FOUR

You Shall Call Your Walls Salvation

Isaiah 60:15–18 *Whereas you have been forsaken and hated, with no one passing through, I will make you majestic forever, a joy from age to age. [16]You shall suck the milk of nations, you shall suck the breasts of kings; and you shall know that I, the LORD, am your Savior and your Redeemer, the Mighty One of Jacob.*

[17]Instead of bronze I will bring gold, instead of iron I will bring silver; instead of wood, bronze, instead of stones, iron. I will appoint Peace as your overseer and Righteousness as your taskmaster. [18]Violence shall no more be heard in your land, devastation or destruction within your borders; you shall call your walls Salvation, and your gates Praise.

Understanding the Word. In these verses we find a recurrence of several of the themes we have encountered earlier in the chapter. Instead of Jerusalem being a source of mockery because of its ruins, now it will be a source of praise because of its splendor. Instead of the nations being a source of oppression and deprivation for God's people, now the nations will be a rich resource for them. (On the figure of nursing at royal breasts, see the commentary notes at the end of the week.) Instead of the common building materials of stone, wood, iron, and bronze, the materials will be iron, bronze, silver, and gold. The point being not only that Judah and Jerusalem will be restored, but that they will be restored to a better condition than they were before destruction. Instead of having wicked, injurious taskmasters, now they will be ruled over by Well-being (see the commentary notes at the end of the week) and Righteousness (v. 17).

Taking a hint from 26:1, Isaiah said of the restored city that its walls are Salvation, and its gates Praise. This gives us a further clue that we are not primarily talking of a prediction that expects literal fulfillment. The City of

God is not so much a place as it is a condition. This is not to say that God in his wonderful plans for the consummation of all things could not somehow involve time and space in those plans. But it is to say that it is wrong to become obsessed, as some are, with precisely how these kinds of statements are going to be worked out in time and space. What is being talked about in these promises is the spiritual abundance, the well-being, the security, and the joy that can be ours when we know Jesus Christ as our Savior and are filled with the Holy Spirit. What God may yet have planned for us in the future is his matter, but whatever it is, we know that it will be beyond compare.

As always in the Bible absolute promises are conditional. That sounds like an oxymoron, but it is not. Isaiah says without qualification that "violence shall no more be heard in your land" (v. 18), but, in fact, violence did reoccur in the land after Israel had been restored in 538 BC. There was Antochus IV who did his best to exterminate Judaism in 167 BC, and then there was the destruction of the temple in AD 70, followed by the leveling of Jerusalem and the complete reorientation of the city in AD 135. So how are we to take Isaiah's words? Were they only intended for the "new Jerusalem coming down out of heaven" (Rev. 21:2), that is, the last days? Or could they have actually described the historic land of Israel in some sense? I think the latter is the case. God makes absolute promises that assume we will be faithful. There is no wishy-washiness in the promises; this is the way it will be. But our faithfulness is never left out of the equation. If we do not respond in faith and obedience, then the entire equation falls apart. But from God's side, it is, and can be, a done deal.

1. How does Yahweh's word to Nineveh through Jonah (Jonah 3:4) give us a positive example of the absolute/conditional nature of God's promises? Can you think of others?

2. Can you think of other examples where spiritual reality is spoken of in physical terms? What about "a clean heart"?

3. If you were going to put Isaiah's promises to Jerusalem in spiritual terms, how would you say it?

FIVE

The LORD Will Be Your Everlasting Light

Isaiah 60:19–22 *The sun shall no longer be your light by day, nor for brightness shall the moon give light to you by night; but the LORD will be your everlasting light, and your God will be your glory. ²⁰Your sun shall no more go down, or your moon withdraw itself; for the LORD will be your everlasting light, and your days of mourning shall be ended. ²¹Your people shall all be righteous; they shall possess the land forever. They are the shoot that I planted, the work of my hands, so that I might be glorified. ²²The least of them shall become a clan, and the smallest one a mighty nation; I am the LORD; in its time I will accomplish it quickly.*

Understanding the Word. In these final words in the chapter, the prophecy moves to an even more lyrical level that it had been previously. Clearly, here, we are talking about last things—the age to come. This is confirmed by the way the Revelation of Saint John clearly makes use of this same language (Rev. 21:22–26). Both passages speak of the wonder of that time when we will no longer need created light, because uncreated Light will manifest itself in undimmed form. No longer will there be any night, and no oppressors will remain, so the gates of that city will never need to be closed (see v. 11 above, and Revelation 21:25). The time for mourning will be over; mourning over injustice and death and oppression will be gone forever. What wonderful thoughts, what a hope to look forward to!

Notice the personal pronouns in verses 19–21. Yahweh is not merely *the* Light, but *your* Light. Nor is God merely glorious, but he is *your* glory. This language is emphasizing once more the profoundly personal relationship God wants to have with us. As the phrase "the Holy One of Israel" speaks of Yahweh's amazing condescension in being willing to belong to the people of Israel, so here he wants to be the Light and the glory of each one of us. What does that mean? For him to be your Light means that he will enable you to recognize his truth and to walk in it. For him to be your glory means that you no longer have to struggle to gain significance and recognition, but can give up that struggle with a sigh of relief, knowing that it is as you give yourself up to God, his reality and honor will invade your life, and you will find your true

84

self in him and in his service. We will be a "shoot" that he has planted (v. 21), one that the world may well call worthless, but one that has eternal worth in him. In that light, each of us will become greater and be worth more than we could ever imagine (v. 22). As God gives his glory to us, we in turn will glorify him; as he makes us more real, our lives will demonstrate his reality more fully.

In this light, the opening statement of verse 21 is important. How do we glorify God? We do so by manifesting his character in our lives, by doing what is right. This is not something we do on our own, thus glorifying ourselves. God plants us and nourishes us, and his character springs up in us as we cooperate with him. Jesus uses a similar figure when he identifies himself as the vine and us as the branches (John 15:1–6). On the one hand, the vine would die if it had no branches, but on the other, the branches are dead if they are cut off from the vine. We live and produce divine fruit only because of our attachment to him, but it is through us that his fruit is picked by the world.

1. What is the great danger in the self-esteem movement?

2. What is the great danger in a theology that says we are only considered by God to be righteous because of Jesus' sacrifice for us, but that we can never actually be righteous in our daily lives?

3. How does God manifest his glory in our lives?

COMMENTARY NOTES

i. Nebaioth and Kedar (Isa. 60:7) are the first and second of Ishmael's sons as named in Genesis 25 (as well as in 1 Chron. 1:29). Thus, their names, and particularly that of Kedar, come to represent the entire region east and southeast of the Dead Sea where Ishmael is said to have settled. This would broadly include Moab, Edom, Midian, and the inhabitable parts of western Arabia (see Isaiah 21:13–17). While there were some villages and towns (Isa. 42:11), many of the peoples of the region were Bedouin herders living in tents (Ps. 120:5; Song 1:5) and noted for their flocks and herds (2 Kings 3:4; Ezek. 27:21).

ii. The figure of nursing at the breasts of royalty (Isa. 60:16) seems to be an adaptation of the figure found in many of the representations of kings in the ancient world, especially in Egypt, where the king is depicted suckling the breast of a goddess. This is, of course, a way of saying that the king has a spark of divinity in him. No Old Testament writer is going to make that application to Yahweh, who is suprasexual and transcendent. But the figure could be adapted to express the idea that former slave Israel will now be cared for by kings.

The apparent contradiction found in the statement "suck the breasts of kings" is fairly easily resolved. "Kings" can be a way of expressing an abstraction, thus "royalty," and the genitive phrase "x of x" can be used to express an adjectival relationship. Thus "the mountain of my holiness" can be rendered "my holy mountain." That means that the clause here is "suck royal breasts."

iii. A particular kind of literature grew up among the Jewish people in the last two centuries before Christ. It is characterized by a number of distinct features, several of which can be explained by what was happening to these people at this time. From 190 BC they had come under the rule of the Seleucid kings from their capital at Antioch. These kings sought to force the Jewish people to adopt Greek customs, many of which were not only repulsive to the Jews, but were actually forbidden by their Torah. This conflict came to a head when one of these kings, Antochus IV, tried to stamp out the Jewish religion by reconsecrating the temple in Jerusalem to Baal and forbidding possession of or reading of the Torah. That effort eventually failed and, in the upshot, the Jews were able to break free from Antioch and establish their own kingdom. But that effort was not a success, because the kings and priests of that kingdom became increasingly corrupt, and eventually fell into internecine warfare. One side asked the Romans for help (64 BC) and, predictably, Rome simply took over. They allowed an Arabian warlord to run the territory for them and he was succeeded by his son (by a Jewish woman) who is known as Herod the Great.

As a result of all of this, the Jewish thinkers could not see much evidence of Yahweh's control of history. Instead, they saw history becoming worse and worse, until finally God's patience would run out, and he would bring time to an end. At that point, he would save his people through his Messiah and would establish his eternal kingdom. Under persecution, this kind of literature, purporting to tell of the overthrow of "the empire," whatever that empire was understood to be, was subversive. Thus it was heavily coded with secret signs, names, colors, numbers, and fantastic imagery, things that only the elite could understand.

It is evident that the New Testament book of Revelation shares many, though not all, of these features. Thus the Greek name of the book *Apocalypsis* came to be used as the category name, apocalyptic, for all this type of literature.

Certain portions of the Old Testament, which some scholars believe share these characteristics, have also been labeled "apocalyptic," including Isaiah 24–27; 60–62; Daniel 8–12; and Zechariah 9–14. However, some of the key features of apocalyptic literature are missing from these, most especially the despair over God's salvation being worked out in history. Also some of the extremes of coding are missing from these passages. To be sure, they do seem to be speaking of the end of time, and they are more image-laden than other Old Testament narratives and discourses. However, I would argue that these examples are speaking of end times (eschatology) in a different way than does typical apocalyptic text.

This has implications for the dating of the Old Testament examples. If these are truly examples of apocalyptic literature, then either they are very late (second century BC), which the apparent dating of the books would deny, or the apocalyptic impulse began much earlier than is generally believed. On the other hand, if we can see them as only eschatological, then there is no conflict with the implied earlier dates of these materials.

iv. Elsewhere in this series I have discussed the Hebrew word *shalom*, often translated "peace," but for convenience's sake, and because of its occurrence here in Isaiah 60:17, I will comment on it again. Like many Hebrew words, *shalom* has a very large pool of potential connotations, which are expressed by several different English words. Thus, it would be incorrect to simply say that *shalom* means "peace." To be sure, in many cases it does mean that, although with a somewhat different flavor than the English word. But in many other cases, it is not correct to translate it with "peace," and I would argue that this is one of those places (see also Isaiah 53:5).

The basic idea of the root *sh-l-m* is to be whole or complete, thus words built on that root can mean "to finish," "to settle" (a debt), "to make whole" (i.e., healthy), "health," "well-being," "to have harmonious relations," etc. Thus, for *shalom* to exist between two persons or peoples is more than a mere absence of conflict, as is often the only connotation of the English "peace." Thus Jesus could say, "my peace I give to you. I do not give to you as the world gives" (John 14:27). Jesus can make us whole, something the world can never do.

In the context here, I believe "peace" does not adequately express what God is promising his people. In the ancient world, and in all too much of the modern world, an overseer or a taskmaster was not guided by what was right for those under him, nor did he have any interest in their well-being. The only interest was to get the maximum of productivity out of them before they dropped dead. But that will not be the case in God's kingdom. There, the overseers *will* be concerned for what is right for those under them and will promote their well-being (e.g., 1 Thess. 5:12–13).

WEEK SIX

GATHERING DISCUSSION OUTLINE

A. Open session in prayer.

B. View video for this week's readings.

C. What general impressions and thoughts do you have after considering the video and reading the daily writings on these Scriptures?

D. Discuss questions selected from the daily readings.

    1. **KEY OBSERVATION:** It is when God's glory is seen in us that the world is drawn to him.

    DISCUSSION QUESTION: What is the evidence of God's glory in people whom the world might call insignificant?

    2. **KEY OBSERVATION:** God has kept his promises to Abraham and his people have not been exterminated (even though it has been tried many times).

    DISCUSSION QUESTION: What does the fulfillment of God's promises for the children of Abraham mean for the fulfillment of his promises for his church?

    3. **KEY OBSERVATION:** The absolute lordship of Jesus Christ will be recognized by every person on earth, but not all will do so voluntarily.

    DISCUSSION QUESTION: If, in the end, persons will no longer be able to deny that Jesus is Lord, why might they still refuse to give him their hearts?

4. **KEY OBSERVATION:** The City of God is not so much a place as it is a condition.

   DISCUSSION QUESTION: If you were going to put Isaiah's promises to Jerusalem in spiritual terms, how would you say it?

5. **KEY OBSERVATION:** God wishes to have a personal relationship with each of us in which his light and glory are *our* light and glory.

   DISCUSSION QUESTION: How does God manifest his glory in our lives?

E. What facts and information presented in the commentary portion of the lesson help you understand the weekly Scripture?

F. Close session with prayer.

Isaiah 61:4–62:12

The Nations Will See Your Righteousness

INTRODUCTION

We come here to the parallel of chapter 60. These two sections are on either side of the climactic revelation of the Messiah in 61:1–3. Chapter 60, the dawning of the Light, was the effect following the cause, namely the Divine Warrior of 59:15b–21. In the case of 61:4–62:12, the effect precedes the same cause, the revelation of the Warrior in 63:1–6. As a parallel to chapter 60, we find several of the same themes repeated here, such as the promise that the foreign oppressors will serve God's people, and that the people will enjoy the abundance of the land in security. But here there is more of an emphasis upon what it is that the surrounding nations will see. Primarily they see two things: they will see how precious Israel is to God (61:9), and they will see God's righteousness being reproduced in his people (61:11). While it is not explicitly said that the nations are drawn to Israel's God because of this, that is the clear implication, especially as this passage is parallel to chapter 60, where that point is explicitly made. In a sense, then, the two passages are related by causation, with chapter 60 giving the effect (the nations coming) with some indication of the cause (God's redemption demonstrated in divine character), while 61:4–62:12 expresses the cause more fully, and assumes the previously stated effect.

The righteous character of the redeemed nation is expressed in a variety of ways. It was already introduced in 61:3, where it was said that the effect of the Messiah's ministry was that his redeemed people would be "oaks of righteousness, the planting of the LORD." So 61:10 says, "he has covered me with the robe of righteousness," and verse 11 "[he] will cause righteousness and praise to spring up before all the nations." In 62:1, "her righteousness [NRSV "vindication," see the commentary on righteousness in Week Three] shines out like the dawn" (NLT), and verse 2 says, "the nations will see your righteousness [NRSV "vindication"]" (NLT). Finally, in 62:12 Israel is called "The Holy People." While this epithet clearly speaks of the nation as being Yahweh's exclusive possession, it is also clear that to belong exclusively to the Holy One assumes that such a person will also reproduce Yahweh's holy character.

One of the important figures of speech expressing the restoration of the relationship between God and his people is the marriage metaphor appearing in 61:10 and 62:3–5. This is significant because of all the places earlier in the book where Israel was depicted as a woman bereft of her husband, either through violence (3:25–4:1) or because he has divorced her (54:6). But whatever the past may have been, God now rejoices over his people as a bridegroom rejoices over his bride.

ONE
Priests of the Lord

Isaiah 61:4–7 *They shall build up the ancient ruins, they shall raise up the former devastations; they shall repair the ruined cities, the devastations of many generations.*

⁵Strangers shall stand and feed your flocks, foreigners shall till your land and dress your vines; ⁶but you shall be called priests of the LORD, you shall be named ministers of our God; you shall enjoy the wealth of the nations, and in their riches you shall glory. ⁷Because their shame was double, and dishonor was proclaimed as their lot, therefore they shall possess a double portion; everlasting joy shall be theirs.

Understanding the Word. There is some question whether verse 4 should be taken with verses 1–3 or with verses 5–7 as here. The reason for the question is that it is not absolutely clear who the "they" of verse 4 refers to. It could be the redeemed people of God, as in verse 3. But it could also refer to the strangers and foreigners of verse 5. I take it as the latter, in part because both verses 4 and 5 speak of the restoration of the land, whether cities or fields. The point is similar to the one made in chapter 60: the ones who once tore down the cities will now assist in their rebuilding, and the ones who once forced the Israelites into menial labor will now take that position on behalf of the Israelites.

But this does not mean that the positions are simply reversed, with Israel now in the position of overlord, able to oppress the former oppressors. No, the former oppressors take the lower positions of builders and laborers so that Israel may finally begin to fulfill the role that should have been theirs from Mount Sinai onward: "a priestly kingdom and a holy nation," (Exod. 19:6). Israel was intended to be the servants of God for the sake of the world. Unfortunately, they got caught up in being a nation state, and it was only when all the trappings of nation statehood had been stripped from them that they were finally able to be recalled to their original role. Priests serve God on behalf of the rest of the worshippers. They are called to be mediators, go-betweens, who introduce the people to God and God to the people. This was to be the function of Israel in the world.

Although the text of Isaiah 6:7 is very difficult (as seen in the variety of translations; see the commentary notes at the end of the week), the overall sense is clear enough. It is a continuation of the reversal theme. Israel had experienced shame and humiliation. It had appeared that the Yahweh in whom they had trusted had failed them, and as a result they had been disgraced. It appeared that their Father had abandoned them. But that, of course, was not the case. It was not God who had failed them; rather, they had failed him. Thus what had happened to them had been perfectly just. And if God had left them in captivity, that would have been just, too. But that is not what had happened. God delivered them from captivity and apparent abandonment, not because they deserved it, but simply as an expression of his love for them. They have been restored to the position of a beloved son. Instead of having no inheritance, they will receive the double portion allotted to the favorite son, the firstborn. Instead of their portion being doubt and depression, it will now be eternal joy.

1. Think of places in your own life where, instead of receiving what you deserved, you received something better, by the grace of God.

2. We as Christians believe in "the priesthood of all believers." If that is true, what are some ways that we can be mediators between God and the world?

3. What are some ways in which you can make it easier for your pastor to carry out the special ministry that God has given him or her?

TWO

A People Whom the Lord Has Blessed

Isaiah 61:8–11 *For I the LORD love justice, I hate robbery and wrongdoing; I will faithfully give them their recompense, and I will make an everlasting covenant with them. ⁹Their descendants shall be known among the nations, and their offspring among the peoples; all who see them shall acknowledge that they are a people whom the LORD has blessed. ¹⁰I will greatly rejoice in the LORD, my whole being shall exult in my God; for he has clothed me with the garments of salvation, he has covered me with the robe of righteousness, as a bridegroom decks himself with a garland, and as a bride adorns herself with her jewels. ¹¹For as the earth brings forth its shoots, and as a garden causes what is sown in it to spring up, so the Lord GOD will cause righteousness and praise to spring up before all the nations.*

Understanding the Word. Like verse 7, verse 8 is also somewhat obscure. Once again, as in verse 4, the antecedent of "them" is not specified. Furthermore, the second clause seems to have a misspelled word in it: where a majority of the versions have "wrong" the Hebrew has "burnt offering" (see the commentary notes at the end of the week). Thus, it is possible that, whereas the original intended to say that the enemies had been guilty of robbery and wrongdoing, a copyist had thought it was the Israelites being referred to and remembering such a passage as 1:13, "I hate iniquity and solemn assembly," changed "wrongdoing" to "burnt offering." However, in this part of the book "recompense" is normally what is given to Israel's enemies, and the "everlasting covenant" was certainly given to Israel (61:8). Thus, Yahweh is here saying, as is found elsewhere in Scripture (Isa. 10:5–11; Hab. 1:5–6; 2:6–8), that although he brought the enemies upon Israel as a way of disciplining his people, those enemies, for their part, simply came to loot and steal, and they would be held accountable for that. I have said repeatedly in this series that *mishpat*, the word commonly translated as "justice" or "judgment," can connote much more than that, namely, God's divine order for life. The opening two clauses of verse 8 illustrate that point: where robbery and wrongdoing exist, there is a lack of *mishpat*. In English parlance, those two behaviors are not normally understood as constituting "injustice," narrowly speaking. But they are clear evidence of the absence of the divine order of life, understanding *mishpat* in its full sense.

Verses 9–11 are united by what the nations will see when they look at Israel. In verse 9 they will see that Yahweh has blessed his people by preserving them and giving them multiple descendants, even though the empires had determined, by means of exile, to erase them as an independent people group. Verses 10 and 11 speak of the deliverance that God has wrought, not only from the power of the empires, but also from the power of sin. That salvation will be so evident and so beautiful that it will be like a wedding couple's adornments. The nations will see it and be moved to join Israel in praising God.

The language of being clothed with "salvation" and "righteousness" (v. 10) reminds us of what Paul says in the book of Colossians when he says that we "have stripped off the old self with its practices" (Col. 3:9) and calls us to "clothe [ourselves] with compassion, kindness, humility, meekness, and patience" (Col. 3:12). (See the commentary notes at the end of the week for further discussion.)

1. Many of us do not think of our salvation in such eloquent and overflowing terms as those used in 61:8–11. What are some reasons for that?

2. How could God's order for life, his *mishpat*, be enhanced in your own behavior?

3. What is the significance of the interrelationship of salvation and righteousness?

THREE
Until Her Righteousness Shines like the Dawn

Isaiah 62:1–5 *For Zion's sake I will not keep silent, and for Jerusalem's sake I will not rest, until her vindication shines out like the dawn, and her salvation like a burning torch. ²The nations shall see your vindication, and all the kings your glory; and you shall be called by a new name that the mouth of the Lord will give. ³You shall be a crown of beauty in the hand of the Lord, and a royal diadem in the hand of your God. ⁴You shall no more be termed Forsaken, and your land shall no more be termed Desolate; but you shall be called My Delight Is in Her, and your land Married; for the Lord delights in you, and your land shall be married. ⁵For as a young man marries a young woman, so shall your builder marry you, and as the bridegroom rejoices over the bride, so shall your God rejoice over you.*

Understanding the Word. The first two verses speak of the Israel that will be seen by the nations. They will no longer see a sinful, yet proud nation, defeated by their sin but yet claiming to be the chosen ones. Instead, they will see a nation out of whom the righteousness of God shines like the dawn (cf. 60:1–3). The NRSV and NIV interpret the meaning differently and consequently translate Hebrew *tsedeqah,* which is normally translated "righteousness," as "vindication." They take it that Israel is defeated by enemy nations and now by being delivered from those nations is shown to have been right to trust God. While that interpretation might have been justified in the context of chapters 40–55, it is not justified here. Israel, as depicted clearly in 56:9–59:15a and 63:6–66:17, is defeated by sin, not enemy nations, and what is manifested is a life of victory over sin. However, it might be argued that "vindication" is justified even on those grounds; namely, that Israel is shown to be right by trusting God to deliver them from the consequences of their sins, while they continue to commit them. This is, of course, a parody of reformation theology. That theology rightly maintains that we are not justified before God by any right behavior that we produce on our own. This was a needed corrective to popular medieval theology that seemed to suggest that we make ourselves acceptable to God by rigorously mortifying our flesh. However, there is a subtle suggestion in that thought that since we are justified (made right with God) by faith alone, therefore there is neither the need for, nor the possibility of, a new life of Spirit-empowered righteousness. This idea is a travesty, one that, if left unchecked, will render North American Christianity powerless.

Now, instead of being a faded garland of human pride (28:1–4) Israel will be a "crown of splendor in the LORD's hand" (v. 3 NIV), humbly demonstrating what God can make of a person who is completely surrendered to him. Now they will have a new name. Instead of being called Azubah and Shemma (Deserted and Desolate), they will be called Hephzibah and Beulah (My Delight Is in Her and Married). In both cases, the issue is relationship. On our own and apart from God we are deserted and desolate, tumbleweeds on a vast prairie. But when we gladly give ourselves into God's hand, knowing how precious we are to him, we find our true value. Notice that the language here is not of Sovereign/subject, but of Bridegroom/bride. God does not consider us to be his subjects, but his beloved, his delight. We are not objects of domination, but precious partners in love.

1. How does seeing yourself as God's bride alter your concept of obedience?

2. How can we continue to emphasize the necessity and the possibility of God-empowered righteousness without minimizing the truth of salvation by grace alone?

3. What is the difference between righteousness produced by human effort, and righteousness that is the result of faith?

FOUR
I Have Posted Sentinels

Isaiah 62:6–9 *Upon your walls, O Jerusalem, I have posted sentinels; all day and all night they shall never be silent. You who remind the LORD, take no rest, ⁷and give him no rest until he establishes Jerusalem and makes it renowned throughout the earth. ⁸The LORD has sworn by his right hand and by his mighty arm: I will not again give your grain to be food for your enemies, and foreigners shall not drink the wine for which you have labored; ⁹but those who garner it shall eat it and praise the LORD, and those who gather it shall drink it in my holy courts.*

Understanding the Word. As chapters 49–52 came to their climax looking for the unveiling of the Lord's mighty arm to overcome the consequences of their sin and restore them to himself, the prophet brought in the image of the watchmen on the walls of a besieged city looking hopefully to the mountains for some sign of the coming of the King at the head of a relieving army (52:7–10). In these verses we see the same images being introduced again. Now it is not deliverance from the consequences of sin that is in view, but deliverance from its power. What will the nations see when they look at Israel? Will they see a people no different from themselves—proud, fickle, liars, adulterers, sensuous? Will they see a people whose "heart [is] not steadfast, whose spirit [is] not faithful to God" (Ps. 78:8)? Or will they see Jerusalem established, renowned through all the earth, as the people of God. Once more the sentinels are looking for the one who is coming, this time bringing people with him from all over the earth (see vv. 10–12).

As in chapter 52, it is again God's "mighty arm," his supernatural power, that will do the work necessary to make Jerusalem truly the City of God, the one envisioned in 1:26–27, "the city of righteousness, the faithful city. . . . redeemed . . . by righteousness." If that could happen, then the people of Zion need never again fear an enemy nation being called in to discipline them. The prophets had told the people in the past that because of their sins, all their labor to build homes and grow crops would be in vain. Enemies would come in and take all that the Israelites had worked so hard to produce (Deut. 28:33; Isa. 1:7; Jer. 5:17). But if the people would be faithful, that need not ever again be the case. As I commented in a previous lesson, in fact, that disaster did happen again. But Yahweh is stating the principle here. It did not *need* to happen again, and in the end, in the age to come, it *will not* happen again. Verse 9 amplifies the principle still further: work and productivity are a gift from God. Those who are living according to God's divine order, his *mishpat*, know that the ability and the opportunity to be productive are made possible only through the grace of God. Thus they eat and drink what their hands have produced with praise and worship to him. The great tragedy is when gifted and productive people take the credit for themselves, failing to understand that all they have accomplished has come from a loving heavenly Father.

1. Why is it often hard for gifted people to cultivate an attitude of gratitude? What happens to us when we take the credit for ourselves for our accomplishments?

2. What is the evidence of a heart established in God and a spirit that is faithful to him?

3. Suppose a person has been faithful to God, and yet the products of their work are stolen by someone else. How do we explain that in the light of the principle discussed?

FIVE

Build up the Highway

Isaiah 62:10–12 *Go through, go through the gates, prepare the way for the people; build up, build up the highway, clear it of stones, lift up an ensign over the peoples. ¹¹The LORD has proclaimed to the end of the earth: Say to daughter Zion, "See, your salvation comes; his reward is with him, and his recompense before him." ¹²They shall be called, "The Holy People, The Redeemed of the LORD"; and you shall be called, "Sought Out, A City Not Forsaken."*

Understanding the Word. The sentinels mentioned in verse 6 see the Victor, the Divine Warrior, the Messiah coming and so they cry out to open the gates. The enemy army, the powers of darkness, are running away and so the formerly besieged people stream out through the gates to begin repairing the ruined highway so that their Deliverer and the host of people with him can come in. The flag of victory is raised to beckon them on. In 11:10 it is said that the Messiah himself will be that flag, calling all nations to himself. So here we have that thought again. Almost certainly, these are some of the passages that prompted Jesus to say, "And I, when I am lifted up from the earth, will draw all people to myself" (John 12:32). But only those intimately familiar with Isaiah 52:13–53:12 would have expected that the flag would be nailed to a cross.

Again, as several times since chapter 35, the language of "reward" and "recompense" appears (35:4; 40:10; 45:13; 49:4; 61:8). Interestingly, the statements in 40:10 and 62:11 are exact duplicates of each other. What is the point? What were the Israelites being repaid for? Was it for being taken into exile? No, for they had richly deserved that; Moses had told them at the very outset that such a thing would happen to them if they forgot Yahweh and worshipped other gods (Deut. 29:25–28). The wonder is that Yahweh was so patient with them, not bringing the disaster on them though they broke his heart for hundreds of years. So what was the reward the Savior was bringing with him? I suggest two things are involved. In the first place, many righteous Israelites, people who loved God and believed in him, were caught up in the whirlwind of the exile. Personally, they did not deserve the pain and tragedy that was coming on the nation as a whole. Though many of them had died in exile, God, in delivering the nation, was rewarding them for what they suffereded unjustly. Second, he was rewarding those who never lost faith during those long, dark years. They continued to believe the improbable words of the prophets that they would go home again, and their faith was being rewarded in restoration to the arms of Yahweh and in the possibility of living out his life before the world. So it is not merely a coincidence that this segment ends with the proclamation that, "They shall be called, 'The Holy People'" (v. 12). They belonged unreservedly to God, to be used for his purposes alone. But more than that, they could do what no dedicated vessel in the temple could do; they could share the holy character of their Bridegroom, and doing so, would draw all the world to him. The city and people who had been divorced ("forsaken") were now desired ("sought after") both by Yahweh and by the world.

1. In what ways can you invite the Victor more fully into the citadel of your heart?

2. Can you think of persons of faith in your family who may now be dead whom Yahweh is now rewarding through you? What are some ways in which he is doing that?

3. Many of us recoil from being called holy, both because we equate it with self-righteousness and because we have set up some impossible standard to which we know we do not live up. But suppose the choice is simply between being unholy or holy? In the light of this study, what does it mean to be a holy person?

COMMENTARY NOTES

i. As mentioned earlier, the Hebrew text of 61:7 is very difficult, resulting in some differing translations. As it stands, the text reads: "Instead of your shame a double portion; and humiliation they will joyously shout their allotment; therefore in their land they will possess a double portion, eternal joy will be on them." One of the issues is the disagreement in pronouns, between second and third plural; however, this kind of disagreement within sentences in Hebrew is more common than most people realize because, as in this case, most English translations harmonize the disagreement. The second issue, the absence of a pronoun before "humiliation," is not so problematic, because it is now generally understood that a pronoun in the first colon of a poetic pair does double duty. So it is quite proper to translate "Instead of your shame . . . ; instead of humiliation." A third issue has to do with the absence of a preposition between "shout" and "their portion." English demands something like "shout *over* their portion." But that is really an English problem; Hebrew, especially in poetry, does not need a preposition, one merely being understood. All this being said, the most likely translation is: "Instead of your shame, you will receive a double portion; instead of being humiliated, they will shout joyously over their allotment. They will inherit a double portion; eternal joy will be theirs." Note that the final clause is a close duplicate of 35:10 and 51:11.

ii. The text of 62:5 is also problematic, primarily because of the oddity in our minds of the apparent assertion that sons will marry their mother (NKJV). This has prompted the suggestion, even though the present Hebrew reading is supported by all the ancient versions, that "your sons" should be corrected to "your builder." This is a very easy change to make, from *banayk* to *bonek* although it also means changing the preceding verb from plural to singular. However, given that the ancient translations all support "sons," and that a harder reading, which "sons" is, is more likely to be original than an easier reading, which "builder" is, it is probable that "sons" is original. That means that we must find a way to understand how "sons" would function in this sentence. It seems to me that the solution is in the direction of the New Living Translation, which reads: "Your children will commit themselves to you, O Jerusalem, just as a young man commits himself to his bride." While the verb is regularly used for marriage, its larger connotation is "to take possession of," and that seems to be the sense in which the sentence is using the term here. This is a repetition of a theme that we have remarked upon previously. Judah need not fear about her continued existence in the future. Her descendants would be many and they would not disassociate themselves from their past and their heritage (see 44:1–5). They will take the city and nation to themselves just as firmly as a groom takes a bride to himself. That word about her descendants is a promise from the Bridegroom to his bride.

iii. The Hebrew term *nes*, "ensign, flag, banner, signal flag," occurs throughout the book of Isaiah and is used in a variety of interesting ways (5:26; 11:10, 12; 13:2; 18:3; 30:17; 31:9; 33:23; 49:22; 62:10). In the majority of cases, it is used as a signal flag. So in 5:26 it is raised to call the enemy nations to rally against Israel, and in 13:3 it is used to call God's "holy ones" (NRSV "consecrated ones") to attack great Babylon, symbol of the world in revolt. Similarly, in 18:3 it is a call for an army to come and judge the nations. In 30:17, 31:9, and 33:23 it is the forlorn banner left when a defeated army or people have all fled.

But it is the occurrences in 11:10, 12, 49:22, and 62:10 that are especially significant. In these cases, it is the Messiah himself who will be the signal flag. He will be the flag that calls the nations to God, bringing the exiled Israelites with them. He is the sign of God's grace, power, and glory. He is the means whereby God can justly restore sinful people to himself, and empower them to live new lives of righteousness. As such, he is the embodiment of the glory which all the nations will come to see (66:18–19). Note that in 66:19 he is now a "sign" that God will place among

the peoples of earth, and not merely a signal flag (cf. Luke 2:12, 34; 11:30).

iv. Another common figure in this book is "highway." "Road" and "path" are also frequent, with "path" often referring to either a good or bad way of life. However, both of those are relatively widely distributed throughout the Old Testament. But "highway" shows an unusual distribution. It occurs once in Numbers, thirteen times in the historical books, and then once each in Psalms, Proverbs, Jeremiah, and Joel, and nowhere else. But it occurs ten times in Isaiah (7:3, paralleled by 11:16; 19:23; 33:8; 35:8; 36:2; 40:3; 49:11; 59:7; 62:10). As in the final occurrence in 62:10, the most frequent use is to speak about the sure progress of God and his salvation in the world (11:16; 19:23; 35:8; 40:3; 49:11). The contrast is when the highways are blocked and/or deserted because of evil (33:8; 59:7). It is to be wondered if Isaiah's experience challenging Ahaz to trust Yahweh on "the highway to the Fuller's Field" (7:3), which was the same spot on which the Assyrian officer thirty-five years later mocked Hezekiah's trust in Yahweh (36:2), explains Isaiah's affinity for the word. In any case he uses it effectively to declare that God is determined that from his side no obstacle shall stand in the way of his saving grace coming to us.

WEEK SEVEN

GATHERING DISCUSSION OUTLINE

A. Open session in prayer.

B. View video for this week's readings.

C. What general impressions and thoughts do you have after considering the video and reading the daily writings on these Scriptures?

D. Discuss questions selected from the daily readings.

1. **KEY OBSERVATION:** While we sometimes complain that we do not get what we deserve, the truth is that we, as Christians, have received much more than we deserve.

DISCUSSION QUESTION: Think of places in your own life where, instead of receiving what you deserved, you received something better, by the grace of God.

2. **KEY OBSERVATION:** Our salvation from God should be the cause of great joy and merriment.

DISCUSSION QUESTION: Many of us do not think of our salvation in such eloquent and overflowing terms as those used in 61:8–11. What are some reasons for that?

3. **KEY OBSERVATION:** Salvation is by grace alone. There is nothing we can do to deserve it. Yet the expected end of salvation is supernaturally empowered righteousness.

DISCUSSION QUESTION: How can we continue to emphasize the necessity and the possibility of God-empowered righteousness without minimizing the truth of salvation by grace alone?

4. **KEY OBSERVATION:** Whether the world knows it or not, they are looking for people whose hearts are established in God and whose spirits are completely faithful to him.

   DISCUSSION QUESTION: What is the evidence of a heart established in God and a spirit that is faithful to him?

5. **KEY OBSERVATION:** God's goal in the world is to create a holy people.

   DISCUSSION QUESTION: Many of us recoil from being called holy, both because we equate it with self-righteousness and because we have set up some impossible standard to which we know we do not live up. But suppose the choice is simply between being unholy or holy? In the light of this study, what does it mean to be a holy person?

E. What facts and information presented in the commentary portion of the lesson help you understand the weekly Scripture?

F. Close session with prayer.

WEEK EIGHT

Isaiah 65

For My Servants' Sake

INTRODUCTION

In this chapter we are faced with the full range of the contrasts that characterize this section of the book: chapters 56–66. In terms of the structure that I have proposed for the division, this is part of the second statement of Israel's inability to defeat sin in their lives. The first statement was in 56:9–59:15a. This one extends from 63:7 to 66:17. The first statement tended to focus on the fact of their sinfulness, while this one reflects a bit more on why this is the case. As we know from Week Four, which treated 63:7–64:12, there was a tendency to try to shift the blame to God. If the people were recalcitrant, it was because God did not care enough about them to force them to repent. Already in that material we saw that Yahweh reacted pretty strongly to such a suggestion, and that response continues here. Their behavior does not stem from any lack of God's reaching out to them. Rather, it is because they do not choose to humble themselves and take the way of genuine contrition.

This thought that contrition was possible, and that if it was truly followed great blessing would occur, was developed briefly in the middle of the first statement of the problem (57:13b–19) and that idea is greatly expanded upon here in this second statement. Those who humbly serve Yahweh will be the recipients of a new heaven and a new earth.

I suggest that these figures of new heaven and earth have three layers of reference, and that there is no clear demarcation among them. Isaiah is here describing the kingdom of God. On one level that kingdom has already come in the life of each believer, and what is spoken of in concrete language here is intended to symbolize the spiritual realities in that life. But on another level, the prophet is speaking about the actual conditions in the millennial kingdom when Christ reigns on a renewed and redeemed earth (Rev. 20:4–6). On yet a third level he is speaking of the remaking of the cosmos after "the first heaven and the first earth had passed away" (Rev. 21:1; see also 2 Peter 3:13). But rather like the way in which Christ telescoped the destruction of Jerusalem and the end of the world (e.g., Mark 13), Isaiah here combines all three of these foci into one.

We might ask why the book does not end on this high note. I think there are two reasons. The first is a characteristic of the book; the author never allows his readers to let a bright future promise blind them to present realities. Those present realities must be dealt with if any of the promises are to be realized, and Isaiah will not let us forget that. The second reason is the focus of the entire section: God's empowerment for righteous living has one overriding purpose: that the world may know him. So chapter 56 began on that note, and chapter 66 ends on it. God's work in our lives is not so that we may live in eternal bliss, but so that together with *all the redeemed* we may see his glory, and in that vision live eternally.

O·N E

I Held out My Hands

Isaiah 65:1–5 *I was ready to be sought out by those who did not ask, to be found by those who did not seek me. I said, "Here I am, here I am," to a nation that did not call on my name. ²I held out my hands all day long to a rebellious people, who walk in a way that is not good, following their own devices; ³a people who provoke me to my face continually, sacrificing in gardens and offering incense on bricks; ⁴who sit inside tombs, and spend the night in secret places; who eat swine's flesh, with broth of abominable things in their vessels; ⁵who say, "Keep to yourself, do not come near me, for I am too holy for you." These are a smoke in my nostrils, a fire that burns all day long.*

Understanding the Word. Yahweh's words in verses 1 and 2a are in response to the plaintive cries found in 63:15, 64:1, and 12. There, the prophet, speaking for the people, begs God to break through the hard surface of their rebellion and bring them to repentance. He is their father (63:16; 64:8); how can he turn a deaf ear to their cries? But God will have none of this. The problem is not with him. He had been revealing himself to his people through all the long years when they had been looking in every direction but at him. He had been reaching out to them in their rebellion all along, and they had stubbornly refused to hear him. If they now come to him and blame him for their inability to do right, they need to stop that and instead take a long look in a mirror.

So what is the problem? Isaiah 59:1–2 expressed the central points of this discussion very succinctly. Yahweh's hand is not too short to save, but it is that their iniquities are a barrier, preventing that saving hand from saving them. But are not these cries for God to break through to them signs that they now recognize the problem and are turning away from those iniquities and reaching out to him? In fact, as 65:2b–5 show, they are not; they want God to solve the behavioral problems among them in their society while they continue to believe proudly that their religious carrying on makes them better than everyone around them (especially those despicable "foreigners" and "eunuchs"; see 56:1–8). The fundamental component in repentance is humility, as the well-known statement in 2 Chronicles 7:14 says: "If my people . . . humble themselves [and] pray . . . then will I hear from heaven."

What is described in these verses is the furthest thing possible from humility, especially as in verse 5, "Keep to yourself . . . I am too holy for you." But what Judean would think that sitting in tombs or eating pig meat would make them holy (v. 4)? As I said in the comments on chapter 57, it is very unlikely that any Judean was actually doing that. Rather, Isaiah here, as there, and also in 66:3, is indulging in dripping sarcasm. Almost certainly these, the religious elite, were seeking to bend over backward to reestablish the religious rituals that had been in abeyance during the exile. We also may be seeing here the beginnings of what was later to become the Pharisaic movement. The sense was that Judah and Israel had gone into captivity because they did not keep the law, especially the ceremonial law, carefully. To prevent that from ever happening again they instituted twelve hundred new laws to prevent any possible breaking of the original 613. They were very proud that they never broke God's laws. But Isaiah says that all that religious behavior is of no value at all, and that, in fact, instead of being a "pleasing odor" to God, as right sacrifices (reflecting a humble and contrite heart) are described (e.g., Exod. 29:18), they are simply acrid "smoke in my nostrils" (65:5).

1. What is the antidote to superficial religious performance?

2. Is informal, anti-liturgical religious practice necessarily better than formal, liturgical practice? Why or why not?

3. What is the part of the individual Christian believer in addressing the ills in our society?

TWO

I Will Not Keep Silent

Isaiah 65:6–10 *See, it is written before me: I will not keep silent, but I will repay; I will indeed repay into their laps ⁷their iniquities and their ancestors' iniquities together, says the LORD; because they offered incense on the mountains and reviled me on the hills, I will measure into their laps full payment for their actions. ⁸Thus says the LORD: As the wine is found in the cluster, and they say, "Do not destroy it, for there is a blessing in it," so I will do for my servants' sake, and not destroy them all. ⁹I will bring forth descendants from Jacob, and from Judah inheritors of my mountains; my chosen shall inherit it, and my servants shall settle there. ¹⁰Sharon shall become a pasture for flocks, and the Valley of Achor a place for herds to lie down, for my people who have sought me.*

Understanding the Word. In this passage we see the first expression of the contrast noted in the introduction. On the one hand, the proud religionists are spoken of harshly (vv. 6–7) but, on the other, those people designated as "my servants" are promised abundant blessings (vv. 8–10). There has been some debate about the precise identity of these servants (see the commentary notes at the end of the week and also Day Three), but it seems likely that the description given in Micah 6:8: "to do justice [*mishpat*], and to love kindness [*hesed*], and to walk humbly with your God" captures the essence of what being his servant entails.

The idea of something being written (v. 6) in a day when writing was both rare and expensive was a way of expressing certainty. Thus the judgment coming upon the proud religionists was inescapable. The use of "repay" is ironic. For the postexilic returnees, it was the former oppressors who were going to be paid back (e.g., 40:10; 62:11). But here it is the returnees who are paid back for what they have done. Once again, this is a direct slap at the idea that having somehow survived the exile, they are entitled to favored treatment from God. That is not the case at all, says Isaiah. Birthright and religious performance account for nothing, and those who think so will reap the unhappy consequences of those wrong ideas. There is more irony in verse 7. The returnees were eager to establish the continuity between themselves and preexilic Israel (see the genealogies in 1 Chronicles 1–9) showing that they were the heirs to the ancient promises. But Isaiah focuses on another continuity, the one between their sins and those of their ancestors. These people are continuing the same manipulative, magical approach to deity (in short, idolatry) that their preexilic ancestors had practiced.

Nevertheless, a faithful remnant did remain, and for them, Yahweh's chosen servants, there would be continuity. They might feel as though they were an embattled few, but God promised that they and their faith would have descendants (v. 9) and that those descendants would be the true heirs of all the promises. The religious elites might go their way, bringing destruction upon themselves (perhaps depicted as rotten grapes in a cluster, v. 8), but the revealed faith would survive whatever judgments might come (the whole cluster would not be destroyed). The two places chosen to symbolize the blessing God will give continue the air of contrast. Sharon was the naturally fertile coastal plain stretching north from Joppa to Mount Carmel. But the Valley of Achor was one of the nearly barren wadis draining down from the central ridge to the Jordan Valley. But it is no matter. When God's blessings are flowing, even the apparently barren places in life can become abundant.

1. How can a passage like this encourage us as we face what looks like a continuing decline of the church in North America?

2. Is there some apparently barren place in your life that God needs to make fertile? How does he want to do it?

3. How can worship of the true God become idolatrous?

THREE

To His Servants He Will Give a Different Name

Isaiah 65:11–16 *But you who forsake the LORD, who forget my holy mountain, who set a table for Fortune and fill cups of mixed wine for Destiny;* ¹²*I will destine you to the sword, and all of you shall bow down to the slaughter; because, when I called, you did not answer, when I spoke, you did not listen, but you did what was evil in my sight, and chose what I did not delight in.* ¹³*Therefore thus says the Lord GOD: My servants shall eat, but you shall be hungry; my servants shall drink, but you shall be thirsty; my servants shall rejoice, but you shall be put to shame;* ¹⁴*my servants shall sing for gladness of heart, but you shall cry out for pain of heart, and shall wail for anguish of spirit.* ¹⁵*You shall leave your name to my chosen to use as a curse, and the Lord GOD will put you to death; but to his servants he will give a different name.* ¹⁶*Then whoever invokes a blessing in the land shall bless by the God of faithfulness, and whoever takes an oath in the land shall swear by the God of faithfulness; because the former troubles are forgotten and are hidden from my sight.*

Understanding the Word. Here the contrast between "you" and "my servants" becomes even more pointed. "You" are evidently the people who have been addressed throughout the chapter, but here they are explicitly defined as having forsaken Yahweh. Once again, as we look at this description of the activities of these people, we are forced to wonder how literally to take what is said. Had they actually left the temple ("my holy mountain") to worship the gods of Fortune and Destiny? If so, perhaps we need to take verses 3 through 5 in a literal sense as well. But 66:3 suggests that it is not the behavior itself that was necessarily wrong but that it was the wrong attitude with which the behavior was carried out that made it wrong. So perhaps we are speaking of people who would consider themselves orthodox, but who, because they are unwilling to surrender to Yahweh's will, are using other means to try to figure out the future in order to manipulate it. Almost certainly those Israelites who cultivated the false prophets before the exile would have considered themselves fully orthodox. All the while God has been calling these people to surrender themselves to him. But they would not listen (v. 12). Thus, the situation is exactly reversed from what they have been maintaining; instead of God not listening when they called, it is they who would not listen when God called. Though the reason why they would not listen is not spelled out here, the larger context makes it clear that he had been calling them to give up their proud, arrogant attempts to manipulate him for their own purposes.

In any case, God says that all those attempts are going to fail. The destiny that they are trying to figure out and control is, in fact, to die by the sword (v. 12). On the other hand, his servants, those who have humbly abandoned all attempts to bend God to their will, are the ones who will be blessed. In language that seems to presage that of the Beatitudes, the prophet said that instead of being hungry his servants will be full. Instead of being thirsty, they will have plenty to drink. Instead of being put to shame, they will rejoice. Instead of wailing in despair, they will sing for gladness. Whereas the fate of the religious elites will cause their names to be invoked in curses, the way in which God's faithfulness will be manifested in the lives of his servants will cause their names to be invoked in blessings ("May the faithful God bless you as he has blessed so and so"). We see here, then, one of the typical reversals of Scripture: the lowly will be exalted, while those who have exalted themselves will be put to shame.

1. Why do we have such a thirst to know the future?

2. What is it about the human predicament that explains the many reversals in the Bible (to die is to live, to lose is to win, to exalt oneself is to be humiliated, etc.)?

3. According to this passage, what is the best way to ensure that our names will be remembered favorably?

FOUR

A New Heaven and a New Earth

Isaiah 65:17–20 *For I am about to create new heavens and a new earth; the former things shall not be remembered or come to mind. ¹⁸But be glad and rejoice forever in what I am creating; for I am about to create Jerusalem as a joy, and its people as a delight. ¹⁹I will rejoice in Jerusalem, and delight in my people; no* *more shall the sound of weeping be heard in it, or the cry of distress.* ²⁰*No more shall there be in it an infant that lives but a few days, or an old person who does not live out a lifetime; for one who dies at a hundred years will be considered a youth, and one who falls short of a hundred will be considered accursed.*

Understanding the Word. As I said in the introduction, this is a vision of the kingdom of God, and it is probably functioning on at least three levels. The first is symbolic, picturing the spiritual realities of the kingdom in the lives of his servants, the people discussed in the previous verses. Then there is the millennial reign of Christ over a redeemed earth (Rev. 20:4–6), and finally there is the literal new heaven and earth spoken of in Revelation 21:1. This idea of a progressively unfolding reign of God on earth is made explicit in the Gospels. On the one hand, Christ proclaimed that the kingdom had come (Matt. 12:28). At the same time, he taught that it was near at hand (Mark 1:14) and called people to strive to enter it (Mark 9:47). Finally, he spoke of the kingdom as the final consummation of all things (Luke 22:18). Thus, "kingdom of God" is a way of speaking of the reign of God, first of all in individual human hearts, but eventually over the whole earth, with all the attendant blessings of his lordship.

Notice the repetition of the idea of "creating" in verse 18. Yahweh is the sole Creator of the universe; this means that he alone can do new things. He is not locked into the way things have always been, as are the gods. So he can enable us to transcend our past. Whatever may have been the case, whatever may have ruled us in the past, he can break those bonds and bring a new, beneficial lordship into our lives. He is the Creator.

The second note here is one of overwhelming joy. Throughout the Bible, that is the note that accompanies God taking his rightful place in our lives. It is the feeling of satisfaction when the last piece goes into place in a jigsaw puzzle. It is the smiles on the face of the bridal couple when the final pronouncement is made. It is the laughter when the hayloft and the granary are full, and the sun is setting. It is the deep assurance of rightness, and fitness, and of having found what you were made for. When we try to sit on the throne of the universe, we condemn ourselves to meaninglessness. For what are we? Did we make ourselves? Can we explain what life is about? But when we put the Creator on the throne, and make ourselves his ministers, his priests, he shows us that we are not his servants, but his friends, indeed, his sons and daughters. Suddenly, everything fits together and we have significance and worth. Rejoice!

But there another note here that gives a still further reason for rejoicing. God has conquered death. Isaiah had intimations of how he was going to do that, while we who live on the other side of the cross, the resurrection, and Pentecost know how he did it. He did it by taking it upon himself, triumphing over it, and making that life available to us through the Holy Spirit. There is cause for joy! As the classic hymn says, "Death cannot keep its prey . . . he tore the bars away!"* This is the point of the figures of verse 20. Death has snatched infants from our arms or cut short life in midstream. In the promise of eternal life, death has been defeated in principle, and in the new age to come, it will not exist. Hallelujah!

1. If we are experiencing the kingdom of God in our lives, what should be the evidence of that, both internally and externally?

2. Where could God's lordship be more evident in your life?

3. Whatever the conditions of your life, if Jesus is Lord, there is reason for joy. What could you do to cultivate that joy in a fuller way?

FIVE

They Shall Not Labor in Vain

Isaiah 65:21–25 *They shall build houses and inhabit them; they shall plant vineyards and eat their fruit.* ²²*They shall not build and another inhabit; they shall not plant and another eat; for like the days of a tree shall the days of my people be, and my chosen shall long enjoy the work of their hands.* ²³*They shall not labor in vain, or bear children for calamity; for they shall be offspring blessed by the LORD—and their descendants as well.* ²⁴*Before they call I will answer, while they are yet speaking I will hear.* ²⁵*The wolf and the lamb shall feed together, the lion shall eat straw like the ox; but the serpent—its food shall be dust! They shall not hurt or destroy on all my holy mountain, says the LORD.*

Understanding the Word. This final segment concerning the promised kingdom of God combines several themes that have been mentioned elsewhere

---

*Robert Lowery, "Low in the Grave He Lay," 1874, public domain.

in the book and in the rest of the Bible. They include: enjoying the fruits of your own labor (62:8–9); long, abundant life (65:20); seeing one's children grow up and take their place in society (54:1–3; 65:9ff); God responding to unspoken requests (Isa. 49:8; Ps. 91:15; Jer. 33:3); harmful forces being pacified and pain and destruction being annulled (11:6, 9); and the serpent eating dust (Gen. 3:14).

All of these are addressing the results of a world gone astray, and the final reference to the serpent, with its clear allusion to the fall in Genesis 3 (something not found in the parallel passage in Isaiah 11), seems to say that this focus is intentional. What has happened as a result of the fall? Above all, it is death, with all its baneful influences. Here, of course, we are not speaking merely of the termination of life on this earth, because as C. S. Lewis has helped us imagine in his *Out of the Silent Planet*, in a world that had not fallen, translation to the eternal plane of existence could be a blessed and joyful event. No, it is sin that has brought the pain and frustration, the awful sense of loss and destruction that surrounds our experience of death. This was not what God had envisioned, as this passage shows us so graphically. He wants a world of satisfaction, fulfillment, accomplishment, continuity of life and work in one's descendants, an intimacy with him in which each knows the other's heart so well that it is not even necessary to voice a request to have it fulfilled, a world where destruction will not follow every construction, where brokenness will not destroy *shalom* at every turn, where Yahweh's *mishpat* will shape every relationship and all conduct, where failure will be unknown.

Could there ever be such a kingdom? Cultures where the Bible is unknown cannot believe so. They cannot imagine any other world than the one we know. There is simply the eternal tension of yin and yang, light and dark, positive and negative. The only hope is to escape into nothingness, to be delivered from the endlessly turning wheel of existence, to escape the pain of desire, and to feel nothing at all. So where did the biblical writers get this remarkable concept of a world of harmony? I suggest that the only satisfactory answer is the one they give us: the transcendent Creator revealed his eternal plan, his *mishpat*, to them.

As I said, we can experience the kingdom of God in germ now, while we wait for its ultimate consummation, both at the end of time and beyond time. Today you and I can participate in God's intended way of life, as we crown him absolute Lord over every part of our lives, as we gladly accept our Groom's wedding ring, as we snuggle into the arms of the Father of all the faithful, as we are washed clean by the blood of the Lamb. No, we are not yet free of all frustration, pain, and loss, but we can know—now—a level of satisfaction, fulfillment, accomplishment, and hope that we could never know in any other way. Praise his holy name!

1. Why are satisfaction, fulfillment, accomplishment, and hope some results of the kingdom of God?

2. How would God's kingdom manifest itself in the life of a local church?

3. Why is it that the kingdom of God is necessary for the healthy functioning of human democracy? Why is that not an oxymoron?

COMMENTARY NOTES

i. In Romans 10:20, the apostle Paul quotes Isaiah 65:1 "to be found by those who did not seek me," in support of his explanation of the Gentile acceptance of the gospel when many of the Jews did not accept it. But, as previously discussed, that does not seem to be the intent of the passage in its context of Isaiah. Paul's interpretation is not out of the question, but it does not seem the most likely. So, is Paul misusing Scripture, or, on the other hand, does Paul's interpretation, coming from an inspired writer as it does, require us to read Isaiah in that way?

While there are not simple answers to these questions, we need to understand that the New Testament writers used quotations from the Old Testament in several ways. Sometimes they used such quotations directly to support what they were saying, as for instance in Matthew's use of Isaiah 7:14 (Matt. 1:22–23). Other times they used the quotations illustratively. That is, they were not saying that this is what the Old Testament meant, but simply using a similar thought or incident to illustrate their point. An example of such a use is Jesus' reference to Jonah's spending three days in the belly of the whale (Matt. 12:40). Finally, there is the allusive use of language from the Old Testament that would have been familiar to their hearers for literary effect. An example is Jesus' use of "rivers of living water" in John 7:38.

While not all would agree with me, I suggest that Paul is using Isaiah 65:1 illustratively. That is, he is saying that in the same way the ancient Judean elites rejected God's overtures to them so that he turned to the supposed castoffs of society, the Jews had also rejected God's overtures.

ii. During the 1970s a popular explanation of the conflicts seen in Isaiah 56–66, especially of the contrast between "you" and "my servants" in chapter 65 (vv. 11–16), was that it was a conflict between the "establishment," who were followers of Ezekiel, and the "free spirits," who were the followers of the hypothetical "Second Isaiah." The supposed followers of Ezekiel where like Ezra, who wanted to enforce the laws of the Torah and supposedly wanted to exclude all foreigners (not just unbelieving foreigners) from the community. They also wanted the life of the community to center around the temple and its rituals. The supposed followers of "Second Isaiah" wanted a much freer, more inclusive interpretation of the Torah, and really couldn't care less about all the rituals. They were inspired by the broad and generous promises found in the anonymous prophet's beautiful writings, which now appear as Isaiah 40–55.

There are three things wrong with this understanding. First of all, it smacked rather too much of what was going on in American society in the 1970s with the clash between the establishment and the hippies. Thus, it looked very much as though it was reading back into the Bible the conflicts of contemporary culture.

The second thing wrong with this interpretation is that we have no evidence at all that such groups as these ever existed, or that if they did exist they cohered around these ideas.

The third problem is that those who adopted this approach had to almost completely reorganize the material to make their hypothesis work. In the upshot, it seems much more likely that the combatants were not organized along such tight ideologically defined lines, but were rather more loosely grouped in terms of their response to God's word as it came to them through Scripture. When we take the material in this way, looking at the chiastic way in which it seems to be structured, there is no need to create hypothetical social groupings.

iii. A literal translation of 65:6–7 reads thus: "Behold, it is written before me: 'I will not keep silent, but I will repay; I will repay into their bosom. Both your iniquities and your fathers' iniquities together,' says Yahweh; 'because they made offerings on the mountains and insulted me on the hills, I will measure into their bosom.'" This is obviously difficult, both because of the absence of a verb in connection with "your

iniquities," and because of the shift in the number of the pronouns. A solution to the first problem is to read the two verses together and take "repay into their bosom" as the verb governing "your iniquities." But that does not solve the pronoun issue. Several translations simply make all the pronouns third person plural (e.g., NRSV and NLT). The problem with this is that it loses some of the immediacy that the mixing of pronouns provides. This is not merely about what "they" have done. It is about what "you" have done.

iv. The kingdom of God is a powerful metaphor in that it speaks of an entity rather than merely a relationship, as does "lordship," for example. It is about God's rule in the world and not merely in individual human lives. The metaphor as used in the New Testament goes back at least as far as the book of Daniel with its vision of a stone that crushes the kingdoms of men and becomes a great mountain filling the earth (Dan. 2:34–35). Daniel interprets this as a kingdom set up by the God of heaven "that shall never be destroyed" (Dan. 2:44). Undoubtedly, when Jesus proclaimed that the kingdom was near at hand, his Jewish listeners were ready for a political entity to be established. That was not the case. It was a spiritual entity that Christ was proclaiming.

But it was an entity. We Christian believers are together members of the kingdom of God and we need to think of ourselves in that light.

Many persons in the late nineteenth and early twentieth centuries expected to see the kingdom come on earth in their lifetimes. They expected the church to establish a Christian society in the world in preparation for the return of Christ. Two world wars put an end to that dream.

But there is a unity among members of the kingdom that continues to need nurtured and developed. It can never be monolithic, but it is an organic whole that needs to be cultivated among us. We are part of each other.

WEEK EIGHT

GATHERING DISCUSSION OUTLINE

A. Open session in prayer.

B. View video for this week's readings.

C. What general impressions and thoughts do you have after considering the video and reading the daily writings on these Scriptures?

D. Discuss questions selected from the daily readings.

1. **KEY OBSERVATION:** It is very easy to mistake superficial religious performance for the genuine article.

   DISCUSSION QUESTION: What is the antidote to superficial religious performance?

2. **KEY OBSERVATION:** It is easy to become depressed and defensive as we see the church no longer in a place of prominence in our society.

   DISCUSSION QUESTION: How can a passage like this encourage us as we face what looks like a continuing decline of the church in North America?

3. **KEY OBSERVATION:** The Bible seems to be full of reversals of what seem like the normal order.

   DISCUSSION QUESTION: What is it about the human predicament that explains the many reversals in the Bible (to die is to live, to lose is to win, to exalt oneself is to be humiliated, etc.)?

4. **KEY OBSERVATION:** When we are experiencing the kingdom of God in our lives, one of the results is a deep sense of joy in spite of circumstances.

   DISCUSSION QUESTION: Whatever the conditions of your life, if Jesus is Lord, there is reason for joy. What could you do to cultivate that joy in a fuller way?

5. **KEY OBSERVATION:** Satisfaction, fulfillment, accomplishment, and hope are results of the kingdom of God.

   DISCUSSION QUESTION: Why are satisfaction, fulfillment, accomplishment, and hope some results of the kingdom of God?

E. What facts and information presented in the commentary portion of the lesson help you understand the weekly Scripture?

F. Close session with prayer.

www.ingramcontent.com/pod-product-compliance
Lightning Source LLC
Jackson TN
JSHW011953260525
84902JS00008B/24